LOST IN
FRANCE

LOST IN
FRANCE

THE REMARKABLE LIFE AND DEATH OF

LEIGH ROOSE

FOOTBALL'S FIRST SUPERSTAR

SPENCER VIGNES

First published by Pitch Publishing, 2016

Pitch Publishing
A2 Yeoman Gate
Yeoman Way
Worthing
Sussex
BN13 3QZ
www.pitchpublishing.co.uk

ISBN 978-1-78531-160-4

Typesetting and origination by Pitch Publishing

Printed by TJ International Ltd, Padstow, Cornwall

Contents

ACKNOWLEDGEMENTS

This book would never have been written had it not been for two people.

First, Dick Jenkins (christened Daniel Cecil Richmond Roose Jenkins, but known to most simply as Dick). It was in 2000 that I received a phone call telling me that Leigh Roose's nephew was still alive and living in Shrewsbury. Dick was 96 years old at the time with a hazy short-term memory. Fortunately, his long-term memory was razor sharp. He told me stories aplenty about Leigh and the Roose family which I taped on a Dictaphone while downing multiple glasses of sherry (I don't even drink sherry, but it seemed like the polite thing to do). Listening back to our conversations, I confess I was guilty of questioning some of the finer points because it had all happened so long ago. The mind can play tricks on a 31-year-old, which I was in 2000, let alone a stalwart of 96. And yet my subsequent research elsewhere substantiated everything that Dick had said. Meeting him kick-started the process which transformed Leigh's story from what would have been a newspaper or magazine article into a book.

The second person has no known name, and here's why. During the First World War various soldiers were assigned the task of keeping their respective battalion diaries up to date. Some chose to write only a sentence or two each day, if that. Others however took to the task with gusto logging as much information as they could – location, orders from on high, details of enemy action, casualties, amusing incidents, commendations for bravery, the lot. Whoever was in charge of the regimental diary for the 9th Royal Fusiliers between late August and October of 1916 belonged firmly in the latter category. His identity went unrecorded, but he's the reason I was able to piece together Leigh's time with the battalion in France and the circumstances surrounding his last known sighting. Chapter One and Chapter Nine of this book are as much the unknown soldier's work as mine.

For providing information and support I would also like to thank Hazel Bailey at Stoke City, Sue Beaumont at Huddersfield Town, David Barber, Dominic Cakebread, Neil Coyte, Allison Dowzell and Arwyn Williams at Wales Screen, Helen Fisher of the Cadbury Research Library at the University of Birmingham, Peter Francis at the Commonwealth War Graves Commission, Ian Garland, Reg Gibbs, Ceidiog Hughes, David Jenkins, Geraint Jenkins, Nick Jenkins, Gil Jones, Rob Mason at Sunderland Football Club, Pam and Ken Linge at The Thiepval Project, Ken Montgomery at YMCA England, Brian Payne, Sue Payne, Olwen Roose Jones, Gordon Lock, Ian Salmon, Ceri Stennett, Neville Southall, Arthur Tapp, Derek Tapp, Gaynor Tinsdale, Vanessa Toulmin, Alex Vignes, Sally Vignes, Paul Wharton and everyone at the Everton Football Club Heritage Society, Aberystwyth Library, Arsenal Football Club, Aston Villa Football Club, the British Film Institute, Cardiff Central Library, the Imperial War Museum (London), Kings College Hospital (London), Manchester Central Library, the National Screen &

Sound Archive of Wales (Aberystwyth), the Public Record Office (Kew), Stoke Library, Sunderland City Library and Wrexham Library.

A big tip of the hat to Pitch Publishing – in particular Paul Camillin, Jane Camillin, Graham Hales and Dean Rockett – for being so easy to work with and helping to bring Leigh back into the public domain after so many years in the wilderness.

Authors couldn't exist without the love, support and understanding of those closest to home, so last but certainly not least thank you to my partner Jane and children Rhiannon and Luca for living under Leigh's long shadow for all these years.

For Rhiannon, and in memory of all the missing from World War One

"Before you go to war, say a prayer.
Before going to sea, say two prayers.
Before marrying, say three prayers.
Before deciding to become a goalkeeper,
say four prayers."

Leigh Roose

Introduction

DEAR reader, you and I should really have become acquainted back in 2007. That was when this book was originally due to see the light of day. The reason why it didn't is the stuff of every author's nightmares.

Picture this. You have been working on a biography about a trailblazing football player and war hero, a labour of love almost eight years in the making. You finish the final manuscript and hand it over to the publisher. They promise the world in terms of marketing and distribution, say how excited they are to be associated with a book that's poles apart from the carefully choreographed 'My Story' claptrap released in the name of so many cossetted modern day players. Then it all goes quiet. Too quiet. You hope everything is in hand, but deep down there's a nagging sense that all isn't what it's supposed to be. The advance you were promised months ago still hasn't materialised. You make phone calls seeking reassurances. It's OK, you are told – this is what happens in between the manuscript being delivered and the finished article hitting the shops. The calm before the storm. But don't worry. Everyone here is really, really excited about your book.

And then, the very same week that it is due for release, your worst suspicions are confirmed.....

The publisher has gone into receivership.

To make matters worse, you hear the news second hand. You call the publisher's offices but nobody is picking up the phones. You seek answers. You *need* answers. None are forthcoming. In the meantime your labour of love sinks without a trace. A few review copies make it out of the warehouse onto the desks of journalists who write glowing reviews about a paperback that will never see a bookshop. In some kind of morally questionable deal which you don't fully understand the rights are later assumed by another publisher who, because your book is old news, literally shelves it. At some stage there's a clear-out in the warehouse and all copies are either binned or pulped. You don't know when this occurred. You're not told anything.

All of this really happened to *Lost In France*, my labour of love. What does such an experience do to an author's state of mind? You don't want to know.

It's at times like these that a degree of perspective comes in handy. To quote Boris Becker after he famously exited the 1987 Wimbledon Championships at the hands of a journeyman Australian by the name of Peter Doohan, "Of course I am disappointed but I didn't lose a war. There is no one dead. It was just a tennis match." How damn true. And, let me tell you, there's nothing like writing a non-fiction book in which the First World War plays a pivotal role to put your so-called troubles well and truly in the shade. Sure, I felt broken, but I also knew once I'd managed to re-secure the rights (which took another eight long years) that I would want another crack at *Lost In France* with a different publisher. It was too good a story not to be told. I also felt as if I owed it to Leigh Roose, the man whose story it was, unknown to modern Britain in the 21st century but a household name in his lifetime. With more information coming to light between 2007 and 2016 about someone who had been dead for almost a century, Leigh didn't exactly seem in a hurry to leave me either. In fact I'd never encountered anyone so hell-bent on raging against the dying of the light from beyond the grave, something you will discover for yourselves during the final chapters of this book.

I have Paul McCartney to thank for first introducing me to Leigh Roose. In 1983 the former Beatle released an anti-war single called 'Pipes of Peace'. It wasn't a patch on 'Yesterday' or 'Let It Be', yet still managed to reach the number one spot in the UK charts. One of the reasons behind its success lay in the memorable video that accompanied the song. Set against the backdrop of World War One, it depicted Allied and German soldiers laying down their weapons in order to play football against each other amid the mud and bomb craters of no man's land.

Being 14 years old at the time, and therefore by nature something of a cynical, cocky know-it-all, the words 'as' and 'if' were never far from my lips whenever this video appeared on our TV screen at home. That was until one evening when my father, patience exhausted, explained (a) that it was based on real events which had taken place on the Western Front during Christmas Day 1914, and (b) I should "belt up" instead of mocking things I knew absolutely nothing about. The following day at school a history teacher who was also aware of the video made a spontaneous decision to devote an entire lesson to the madness of Christmas Day 1914. We learned that there hadn't been one game of football, but several. The soldiers had exchanged gifts and cigarettes, taken photographs of each other, sung songs, even put up makeshift Christmas trees. Within days they'd all returned to their rat-infested trenches and started killing each other again. As a teenager I couldn't work out if this said more about the futility of war or mankind's love of football. I still can't.

Many years later, and by now working as a journalist, I received a phone call from a contact asking if I was interested in writing an article about a Welsh international footballer who had played in one of these Christmas Day matches. The player's name was Leigh Roose and he had kept goal for several leading clubs including Stoke City, Everton, Sunderland and Arsenal over a 12-year period leading up to the First World War.

Driven by the memory of McCartney's 'Pipes of Peace' video, I went off to do some digging only to discover that I'd been sent on a wild goose chase; Leigh Roose hadn't been in the trenches during December 1914 and so couldn't have played in any Anglo-German kick-around. At that point many freelance writers, strapped for time and money, would have dropped the story and moved on. However, something made me continue to dig. And the deeper I went, the more Leigh got under my skin.

Forget about Christmas Day on the Western Front – the truth was even more fascinating. Here was a man, one of the most recognisable sporting faces in Britain during the early years of the 20th century, whose unconventional yet groundbreaking style of goalkeeping had forced the Football Association into making one of the most important rule changes in the game's entire history. Throw in his outrageous sense of humour (especially by Edwardian standards), a playboy lifestyle, the mother of all controversial playing careers plus the mystery and heartache surrounding his death, and gradually it began to dawn on me – I'd stumbled upon a great story, and an untold one at that.

As my initial research between 1999 and 2006 revealed, surprisingly little has ever been published about Leigh considering the significant impact that he had on the evolution of association football as we know it. A handful of authors, namely Peter Corrigan, Nick Hazlewood, Geraint Jenkins and Roger Hutchinson, have touched on his career and colourful personal life in books covering the broader subjects of goalkeepers, Welsh football and Sunderland Football Club. As a player who bucked the Edwardian trend of turning professional by remaining an amateur, free from the constraints of contracts and therefore able to turn out for whatever team he liked, Leigh's name also crops up in several club histories. But that's about the sum total of it which is why piecing together his life took so long. Thank heavens for libraries. If the penny-pinching powers that be get their way and close many of them down then it will be the death knell for books like this devoted to colourful people from the pre-jet, let alone the pre-digital, age. You can only discover so much on the internet. And even then a fair percentage of it is wrong. Trust me.

So here it is, *Lost In France*, resurrected from the dead, given a major overhaul, brought up to date and released at long last by the publisher that I really should have gone with in the first place. If ever a book deserved a second chance then this is it, even though I say so myself. Leigh, I only hope I've done you justice.

Spencer Vignes
Cardiff, Wales
June 2016

THE FIRST HALF

FROM THE CRADLE TO THE SAVE

1

No Man's Land

IT was 1.35pm on Saturday 7 October 1916. After 99 consecutive days of fighting in some of the grimmest conditions imaginable, the Battle of the Somme had degenerated into a futile stalemate with neither side able to gain any kind of territorial advantage over the other.

In a muddy trench west of the small French village of Gueudecourt, the men of the 9th Royal Fusiliers were gearing themselves up for a large scale Allied assault on enemy lines. Morale was low. The attack had been due to take place two days earlier only to be postponed at short notice due to poor weather conditions. Since then heavy German shelling had resulted in 117 casualties, the sheer intensity of the bombardment resulting in several others going down with shell shock.

Struggling under the weight of sodden uniforms and 100 extra rounds of ammunition per Fusilier, all were agreed on one thing: if it was this bad in the trenches, God only knew what fate awaited them in the wide open spaces of no man's land.

From soldier to soldier the message '10 minutes to go' was passed down the line. In these surroundings '10 minutes to live' seemed more appropriate.

In terms of personnel the 9th was no different to many other battalions serving on the Western Front that autumn. Formed in August 1914 in the London suburb of Hounslow, it consisted of young men from all walks of life who had answered their country's call in its time of need – bakers, bankers, bus drivers, ordinary people playing their own small part in a major world conflict. However, in July 1916 they had found themselves fighting alongside one of Edwardian Britain's more extraordinary characters. Leigh Richmond Roose had joined the regiment following almost two years in France, the Mediterranean and Gallipoli with the Young Men's Christian Association (YMCA) providing pastoral, practical and social support to soldiers.

There wasn't a man in the 9th that hadn't already heard of Leigh, the finest goalkeeper of his generation and on the wanted list of virtually every football club in the country. A born showman so good at his position on the field of play that the sport's governing body had been forced to change the laws of the game just to keep him in check. To large chunks of the British male population he was, in short, a legend.

At 38 years of age Leigh was regarded as something of a father figure by his brothers-in-arms in the 9th, many of whom were young enough to be his sons. Standing six feet tall with broad shoulders, he was everything they dreamed of being: athletic, intelligent, famous, popular with the ladies, entertaining company if occasionally a little eccentric. He was also extremely brave. Within days of arriving on the Western Front, Leigh had taken part in an attack on an enemy position known as Ration Trench. The assault had been planned in a hurry and it showed. After 36 hours of heavy fighting, the Germans mounted a counter-attack led by soldiers using *flammenwerfers* – flamethrowers that belched jets of petrol. Leigh had been in a deep, covered trench known as a 'sap' at the time but managed to escape to safety choking on fumes and with his clothes burned. Despite his injuries he refused medical attention and continued fighting until the following morning, throwing grenades until able to lay his hands on a spare rifle. On 28 August 1916 he was awarded the Military Medal for gallantry along with seven other soldiers from the 9th at a hastily convened service in Agny, being promoted to the rank of Lance Corporal in the process.

At 1.39pm three officers began moving along the trench reminding each man of the attack's exact objectives and to "use your bayonets." Haversacks were pulled on and rifles unwrapped from rags designed to prevent them from clogging up with mud. For the smokers in the ranks there was just about time for one final cigarette before zero hour. Up above, the sound of artillery filled the sky. The assault would be assisted by what was known as a creeping barrage, the Allied guns co-ordinated to move with the soldiers across no man's land into German-held territory keeping the enemy bottled up for as long as possible. Because of this there would be no period of silence just before the troops went over, as was often the case.

With 60 seconds to go the first soldiers started to mount the man-made footholds in the trench wall ready to go 'over the top'. Those immediately behind them prayed, exchanged a few words of encouragement and made sure their bayonets were securely fixed. One or two joked that they couldn't wait to get out into the open, so strong was the stench of vomit.

At 1.45pm precisely the officers in the trenches blew their whistles to signal the start of the attack. Shouting with a mixture of fear, rage and grim determination, Leigh and his comrades climbed into the open and hurled themselves towards the German trenches.

At 2.33pm a phone call came through to Brigade Headquarters saying the first objective, the taking of a German position called Bayonet Trench, had been achieved with the loss of around 30 casualties. Seven minutes later another call reported that the second and final objective, an area running parallel and to the south of Barley Trench, had also been reached and that German prisoners were being escorted through Gueudecourt. This appeared to substantiate an earlier message received from Major Maurice Coxhead of the 9th who said that a wounded man had told him things were "going splendidly."

In fact nothing could have been further from the truth. The Allied bombardment had completely overlooked a trench containing four German machine guns situated on the left flank of the planned assault, the area earmarked for attack by the 9th. Leigh's battalion hadn't stood a chance, many soldiers being shot before they had managed to advance a few feet. Elsewhere the 8th Royal Fusiliers (which along with the 9th, the 7th Royal Sussex and the 11th Middlesex Regiment made up the 36th Infantry Brigade) had initially enjoyed some success attacking a more central enemy position with one group of soldiers even managing to get inside Bayonet Trench. However, without the support of the 9th on the left flank they had been forced to retreat.

Confusion reigned. As the light began to fade two things were abundantly clear. One, the attack had failed. And two, the 9th had suffered massive casualties. A head count showed four of the regiment's officers and 21 of its ranks to be dead, with another officer and 131 ranks wounded. But the more telling statistic was the number of missing – four officers, 161 ranks.

Under cover of darkness a handful of survivors managed to crawl to safety having taken refuge in bomb craters. By morning over 150 men remained unaccounted for including Leigh. Ironically his relatives had already given up hope of ever seeing him alive again having been told in 1915 that he was missing presumed dead on the Gallipoli Peninsula in Turkey.

It would be another 87 years before Leigh's family finally discovered what happened to him that grisly October afternoon.

2

No Place Like Holt

IN north-east Wales, football rules. It always has and probably always will. Forget about rugby union, traditionally the preserve of the old industrial heartlands of the south. As far as most people in Flintshire, Denbighshire and Wrexham are concerned the round ball game (often referred to as soccer to avoid any confusion with rugby football) is king.

Journey into this picturesque corner of Britain, where Wales rubs shoulders with the English counties of Cheshire and Shropshire, and you will discover that just about every town or village seems to have spawned a football hero. Ian Rush from St Asaph, Michael Owen from Hawarden, Gary Speed from Mancot, Billy Meredith from Chirk, Mark Hughes from Ruabon to mention a few; famous names who more often than not grew up dreaming of donning the red shirts of Liverpool and Manchester United rather than the ones worn by the Welsh rugby union team. Men who realised those dreams, and then some.

Five miles east of Wrexham on the border with England lies Holt; population circa 1500, pubs two, shops six including one which up until 2006 served as a florist owned by Paul Burrell, one time butler to Diana, the Princess of Wales. Situated on the west bank of the River Dee, Holt has become over recent years a popular commuter village for professionals earning their crust in nearby Chester and Merseyside. Young families want to live there because crime levels are low, the local schools are good and, above all, it's peaceful.

It wasn't always this way. During the second half of the 19th century Holt developed something of a reputation on both sides of the border for two things – unemployment and violence. Outside the summer months, when the strawberry crops of the fertile Cheshire Plain needed picking, there was simply very little work to be had, especially for men. Rather than live in abject poverty many upped sticks and made for the burgeoning industrial centres of north-west England, to places such as Liverpool and Crewe with their docks and railway workshops respectively. Those that stayed found an outlet for their frustrations in the mass brawls that would break out around the village most Sunday evenings. With alcohol consumption outlawed in Denbighshire and Flintshire on the Sabbath, groups of men would travel from far and wide to Holt, leaving their carts and carriages on the Welsh side of the border before crossing the Dee to drink in the pubs of Farndon on the English bank of the river. Afterwards, fuelled up to the eyeballs with ale, they would return to Holt and fight – man against man, village against village, England against Wales. It was, as one local remembers his grandfather telling him, "a bloodbath."

Quite what Richmond Leigh Roose made of Holt when he arrived to take over as minister of the local Presbyterian church in 1877 we can only guess. Richmond, a tall Anglesey-born man with a long, distinguished flowing beard, had spent the previous nine years in a similar position at a church in Hay-on-Wye, 90 miles to the south. He and his wife Eliza had been happy there and weren't too thrilled at the idea of uprooting their young family. However, duty called, and Holt needed a new minister.

On the evening of 26 November that same year, Eliza gave birth to the couple's fourth son in one of the upstairs bedrooms at The Manse, their home adjacent to the church in Castle Street. Family folklore has it that they were stuck for a name for the baby having already used their favourite boys' names – John, Edward and William – to christen the previous three. It was Eliza who came up with a solution, switching her husband's first and middle names around to create Leigh Richmond Roose. After some initial reservations on the part of the father, they finally had the name registered the following January.

Leigh was born into a rapidly changing world, with 1877 in particular proving to be a year of 'firsts'. In July Alexander Graham Bell launched the first telephone company, serving rich businessmen in the north-eastern cities of the United States of America. Earlier the same month the inaugural Wimbledon tennis championships had got under way in south-west London, sport having already made the headlines in March with England's cricket team facing Australia in the first ever Test match between the two countries. Before the year was out Thomas Edison would have recorded sound for the first time on a new invention of his called a phonograph.

Even Holt had begun to move with the times. In 1855 the Reverend Ebenezer Powell and his wife Mary Anne opened Holt Academy, a school directly opposite The

Manse with a broad curriculum including English, French, arithmetic and art. By the time Leigh started attending lessons in 1882 the school had over 80 students, the majority being boarders from all over north Wales and Cheshire. The students brought with them outside influences including one that proved to be an instant hit with local men of all ages – football. The village even spawned its own side, Holt Nomads, which frequently made round trips of up to 200 miles to play friendlies against other clubs.

In 1879 Eliza gave birth to a fifth child, a girl they called Helena. Although the labour process went according to plan, the pregnancy itself was anything but straightforward with Eliza frequently complaining of aches and pains, ones she hadn't experienced while carrying her previous four children. These continued well after Helena had been born, eventually becoming so bad that she sought the opinion of a doctor. A series of tests followed, the results of which confirmed her biggest fears – she had cancer. Eliza died at home on 11 June 1881 aged just 35.

It says much about Richmond Roose's courage, faith and inner strength that life at The Manse in the years after Eliza's death continued very much as it had when she was alive. Supported by Annie Blackwell, the family's domestic servant, together with kind-hearted local souls, Richmond did his level best to ensure that the needs of his children were catered for.

The house and its surrounding garden remained one of the focal points of the community and continued to do so right up until his death in 1917. "There was always something going on there," remembered the late Arthur Tapp, in his nineties when interviewed during 2000, who was born in the village and baptised by Richmond. "If the church was being used for a wedding, then the gathering afterwards would happen at The Manse. In the spring and summer there would be get-togethers where anyone could come along and mingle, have something to eat and relax. It was a great place for us kids to play and we were always made to feel welcome there."

Richmond's 'open house' policy ensured that his children came face to face with a raft of people belonging to different social, economic and political backgrounds, from eminent members of the religious order to publicans, school teachers to grave diggers. Many years later the Sunderland and England forward George Holley would remember Leigh as the kind of person "who could put any man at ease with his company," a personal quality that probably owed much to his upbringing at The Manse.

One name almost certainly on the guest list for gatherings at the house would have been Herbert George Wells, better known today as H G Wells. Before embarking on a writing career that produced such classics as *The War of the Worlds* and *The Time Machine*, the father of science fiction spent a year working as a teacher at Holt Academy. Whether he would have bothered attending any of the Roose family functions is, however, debatable as Wells grew to hate the village and its people, in particular the Academy headmaster James Oliver Jones.

'From the first few weeks, I knew I should have to escape from this flat, grey, desolate land, the dirty school and its Presbyterian habits', Wells later wrote. 'Holt turned out to be a squalid ill run travesty of the word "Academy"where boys slept three in a bed, lessons took place with the uncertainty of April showers, and downright disorder threatened with such persistence that the headmaster freely advocated in private the physical punishment that he abhorred in public'.

Wells also noted that there seemed to be 'an inordinate quantity of football to fill the gaps between learning'. Part of his teaching duties included refereeing matches between the boys, albeit reluctantly and without appearing to know the rules. It was during one of these games that he slipped on the muddy ground and was kicked hard in the back by Edward Roose, one of Leigh's elder brothers. It proved to be the final straw and Wells left a matter of weeks later after the kidney ruptured by Edward's boot had healed. Nobody ever did establish whether the kick was intentional or accidental.

If the athleticism and drama of this relatively new sport was lost on Wells, it certainly hadn't escaped the young Leigh Roose. Inspired by the thrilling tales of FA Cup finals and international matches told by boarders at the Academy and visitors to The Manse, he was busy playing as much football as possible. Like any concerned father, Richmond insisted his son's schoolwork came first (Leigh was always among the brighter pupils in his classes) while Sunday remained a day of rest. Attendance on family trips to places such as Lake Bala and the north Wales seaside resort of Rhyl was also mandatory. But by the age of 11 large chunks of Leigh's time both inside and outside school were spent with a ball at his feet.

Within a couple of years, that had begun to change. Like most footballers of any standard, Leigh had initially been drawn to the game as a child by the idea of kicking a ball into a net. Yet as time went by he found himself attracted to the one position on the football field where the player was free to handle the ball – that of goalkeeper. Created specifically to act as a last defender, the role of goalkeeper had only been embraced by the Football Association (the sport's governing body in the UK) as recently as 1871. Up until then teams had usually played with nine attackers and two defenders, with each side abiding by what was known as the 'fair catch' rule. This allowed any player close to the goal to catch the ball and take a free kick providing they made a mark in the pitch with their boot, similar to the rule still observed to this day in rugby union.

With hindsight it's easy to pigeonhole anyone wanting to become a goalkeeper around this period as being completely crazy. They were, to put it bluntly, on a hiding to nothing, largely unprotected by referees and regarded as cannon-fodder by outfield players who developed a practice known as 'rushing' to deal with them. This involved one or more players using physical means to 'take out' the goalkeeper, giving a teammate the opportunity to score. Bones were broken, heads split and very occasionally someone died. The Scottish international Teddy Doig, a predecessor of Leigh's between the posts at Sunderland from 1890 to 1904, recalled how the West Bromwich Albion and England forward Bill Bassett once prevented him from reaching a loose ball by sitting on his head. On another occasion Doig was sent flying by a punch from Aston Villa's Harry Hampton while defending a corner kick. However, he managed to exact some revenge by rising to his feet, pinning Hampton to a post and hitting him with an upper-cut before clearing the ball.

Despite the risks it is easy to see why Leigh took to the position like a duck to water. As a teenager he was tall and powerfully built, rising to 5ft 10in by the time he was 15 years old, and would have had no problem whatsoever looking after himself during school kick-abouts. Though popular with his peers, Leigh was equally happy spending time in his own company. At university some went as far as calling him a loner, a description many goalkeepers of subsequent eras might identify with. Years later Leigh himself wrote, 'In other positions in the field, success is dependent on combined effort and the dovetailing of one player's work with another. With the goalkeeper, it is a different matter entirely. He has to fill a position in which the principle is forced upon him that it is good for a man to be alone'.

At 16, Leigh was ready to leave Holt Academy having excelled in all areas with the exception of Greek, a subject he despised. By now he had set his heart of pursuing a career in medicine. Football remained very much an amateur sport. Making a living out of it wasn't something he even considered, no matter how promising a player he was. When the University of Wales offered him a place to study science at its campus in Aberystwyth, Leigh didn't have to think twice. The only problem on the horizon was money, or more specifically a lack of it. Although middle class and comfortably off in comparison with the majority of Holt residents, the Rooses were far from wealthy. Richmond had struggled to send his eldest son John to Oxford University (John would end up following in his father's footsteps by becoming a church minister). Yet any potential hardship would be offset by there being one less mouth to feed at the dinner table every evening. Leigh started classes at Aberystwyth two months after his 17th birthday.

Study may have been the number one priority but there was another reason why Leigh was so keen to take up his place at what, in Wales, is known as 'the college by the sea'. Though damned by some as little more than a chapel-obsessed backwater (the Welsh-born writer Goronwy Rees, later exposed as a Soviet spy, went as far as calling it 'a theocratic society, ruled by priests and elders') the university was fast developing a reputation for sporting excellence. And it had a football team. Leigh joined up immediately, eager to put the skills honed during his youth in Holt to good use.

In truth, Leigh didn't have much competition for the goalkeeper's jersey. The majority of Aberystwyth's 450 or so students, split roughly 50/50 between men and women, came from rural areas across the Principality as yet untouched by the football revolution sweeping the UK. The north-east corner of Wales had succumbed years earlier with Wrexham staging the country's first international match in 1877 and the town's club side winning the inaugural Welsh Cup the following year. But south Wales remained almost exclusively rugby territory, something that would only start to change during the early years of the 20th century with the influx of workers from northern England and Scotland into the region's coalfields and ports.

Leigh, nevertheless, made the position his own. And it was clear from day one that he was very good. His style of play was also completely different from any other goalkeeper of the time. Here was someone prepared to take on menacing centre forwards at their own game, rushing out to break up opposing attacks by whatever means possible – diving on the ball, kicking it clear, or resorting to more brutal means such as clattering into a player with his six-foot frame. Up until then, this just hadn't happened.

Goalkeepers were supposed to stay on or at least near their goal line at all times, daring to venture out only on rare occasions. Not Leigh, who spent long periods of each match playing in the position known today as sweeper, tidying up every loose ball in the gap immediately behind his defenders. Unbeknown to them, those spectators that gathered on the college playing fields were, in effect, watching the forerunner of today's modern goalkeeper in action. As George Holley put it, "He was the mould from which the rest were created."

Leigh's reflexes were astonishing and he could punch the heavy brown footballs used in Edwardian days further than many of his opponents were able to kick them. Then there was his very own secret weapon, bouncing the ball all the way up as far as the halfway line before punting it towards the opposition goal with one of his monstrous trademark kicks. This was perfectly within the letter of the law, though few goalkeepers risked doing it for fear of either leaving their goal unattended or being steamrollered by a centre forward. It became a highly effective, direct way of launching attacks and Leigh used it to his side's advantage whenever possible.

Occasionally, things didn't work out as planned. In one University of Wales inter-college match between the Aberystwyth and Bangor campuses, Leigh had bounced the ball almost as far as the halfway line when he was knocked to the ground by an opposing player. Climbing to his feet, Leigh kicked out at the Bangor man, sparking a mass brawl that left him nursing several cuts and bruises.

Within a short space of time, Leigh became the unrivalled star of the Aberystwyth University side. Attendances rose as word of his remarkable talent spread. Puerile regulations preventing the mingling of the sexes at the Vicarage Fields ground were ignored as female students, drawn by the goalkeeper's good looks, came to watch him play. Revelling in his new-found celebrity status, Leigh would playfully flirt with them before, during and after matches. Free from the constraints of his father's relatively strict domestic regime, he began dating girls for the first time. He also discovered another new 'vice' – alcohol – through regular visits with teammates to The Central Hotel in Portland Street, now an upmarket coffee shop.

Besides openly flirting with girls, Leigh's behaviour on the football pitch began to change in other ways during that first year at Aberystwyth. In an era when players walked sedately on to the field of play, Leigh chose instead to run, acknowledging any applause with either a raised arm or by clapping in return. On reaching the goalposts he would embark on a bizarre ritual, pacing from one side of his penalty area to the other muttering to himself as he went. Was it some kind of mantra, or all part of his act? Nobody knew. But it all helped add a little mystery to the growing enigma that was Leigh Richmond Roose. Some cynics argued that was exactly what he intended.

"He was something of an exhibitionist," recalled Dick Jenkins, Leigh's nephew and only child of Helena Roose, when interviewed in 2000 aged 95 (he would live until shortly before his 103rd birthday). "It didn't matter whether he was playing in front of thousands of spectators or just a couple of people in the back garden. He would always play to a crowd. He saw himself as an entertainer."

At the beginning of May 1896 the entertainer and his side travelled to Liverpool to play against University College, later to become the University of Liverpool. The match was played in conditions more akin to winter than late spring with driving rain falling throughout the day. Among the spectators was Edward Roose, the second eldest of the Roose children, who had journeyed from Holt for the game. Afterwards both Leigh and Edward returned to The Manse for dinner. It was by all accounts an evening to remember with Leigh regaling everyone present with tales of college life and goalkeeping.

The following afternoon Leigh caught the train back to Aberystwyth leaving Edward battling the early stages of a cold, one he apportioned to standing in the Liverpool rain watching the game. Over the next few days his condition gradually worsened until he developed hypothermia. Rather than be transferred to hospital, Edward was cared for at home by the local doctor with Richmond and Helena acting as round-the-clock nurses. He never recovered, dying on 29 May aged just 21.

There's no doubt that the Leigh Roose who eventually returned to Aberystwyth after the funeral was a more subdued version of the one that had wisecracked his way through the previous 15 months at college. In time, elements of the old prankster would once again emerge. Yet Edward's death helps explain why Leigh came to be regarded as something of a Jekyll and Hyde character around the corridors of the university during the remaining three years of his course. Jekyll took the form of a flamboyant athlete who enjoyed the attention of women and a drink with friends. Hyde was the self-possessed outsider, at odds with his latter day reputation as a man of the people, who would rather read a book than attend any of the at-home gatherings that featured so prominently in the diaries of students and staff alike. While Leigh's inability to speak Welsh may have contributed to this, the common consensus within college circles was that he simply couldn't be bothered.

On the rare occasions when he did grace the college's intellectual social circuit, Leigh nevertheless made his presence felt. During one debate he won thunderous applause by vigorously opposing the motion that athletics was 'detrimental to the best interests of the nation'. In February 1899 he was even talked into appearing in a mock trial. Cast as a policeman, his sole contribution was to roar the line 'Silence in court!' He did so with such feeling that many present believed it was the highlight of the evening.

In the autumn of the same year, with his goalkeeping exploits continuing to wow spectators at college matches, Leigh was asked by Aberystwyth Town Football Club if he would be prepared to play for them. Town's first-choice goalkeeper, Jack Jones, had been poached by Manchester City and they needed a replacement. Keen to play at the highest level and mix with 'real' people away from the cossetted student scene, Leigh jumped at the chance.

Town, who shared Vicarage Fields with the college side, were an ambitious amateur club that had recently been forced to leave the Welsh League because of escalating travel expenses, not to mention difficulties in finding players willing to spend hours travelling from isolated Aberystwyth to all corners of Wales. For the 1898/99 season they had turned their attention to cup competitions and friendlies, organising matches against anyone who would play them from village sides to mighty West Bromwich Albion. Leigh made his debut that October in a 6-0 win over the Shropshire outfit Whitchurch. He made a few good saves and employed the same tactics that had served the university side so well, venturing out of his goal with the ball and, whenever possible, appearing to play as an extra defender. For those spectators that hadn't already seen him in action, this took some getting used to. But as the clean sheets (games completed without conceding a goal) piled up, so any murmurs of discontent faded away.

In December Town were drawn at home in the first round of the FA Cup against the professional side Glossop of the Midland League. They won 1-0 with Leigh putting in yet another outstanding performance. In his autobiography *Atgofion Cardi* (Memoirs of Cardiganshire) the Welsh historian Tom Richards, in the crowd that day as a young boy, wrote that Glossop's 'dreams were ended by that wonderful goalkeeper Roose, particularly by his diverting a penalty into the middle of the gorse on Buarth Hill. I saw him play dozens of times afterwards, but never with greater zest and effect than that first time at Vicarage Field'. The mini cup run was ended in the next round by Stockport County but Town, and Leigh in particular, had made an impression.

In the summer of 1899 Leigh finished college having passed his science preliminary exams. He still wanted to be a doctor, intending to attach himself to a hospital where he would be able to study for a degree in medicine. However, that would mean walking out on Aberystwyth Town and his regular girlfriend, a local woman by the name of Catherine Lewis. With time on his side (he was still only 21) and club officials willing to pay generous expenses, Leigh agreed to stay for another year.

It was to prove a wise move. Having secured a place in the North Wales Combination League, Town embarked on what would become the most successful season in their entire history. Cup matches remained a priority and the club entered as many competitions as the fixture list would allow. Leigh was once again on top form, to the extent that calls were made for him to be included in the Welsh side for the Home International Championships (the annual competition between England, Scotland, Wales and Ireland – or latterly Northern Ireland – which ceased in 1984) of 1900. Though keen to play for his country, Leigh was reluctant to do so at the expense of his club which, he couldn't help but notice, had a cup tie scheduled for 3 February, the same day Wales were due to play their opening game against Scotland at Aberdeen. In the event he was spared the dilemma of having to choose between club and country when Blackpool goalkeeper Fred Griffiths was named in the squad. Confident that his big chance would eventually come, Leigh swallowed his pride and focused instead on the relatively mundane world of the Towyn Cup.

Just three weeks later, that chance duly arrived. Griffiths had a nightmare in Aberdeen, making a string of mistakes as Scotland cruised to a 5-2 win. In a bid to turn things around (Wales were already regarded as the whipping boys of Home Nations football, the Scotland defeat being their eighth on the trot), the Football Association of Wales named Leigh as their goalkeeper to face Ireland in Llandudno on 24 February. Also in the squad was a man already on his way to becoming a bona fide star of Welsh football. With his spindly legs, drawn face and moderate pace, Billy Meredith looked anything but one of the most exciting players of his generation. Yet the statistics help tell a different story. By the time he retired in 1924, just a few months short of turning 50, Meredith had played almost 1,600 matches scoring 470 goals in the process and winning 48 caps, an incredible number considering the international fixture list consisted of three annual games against each of the Home Nations. He also won a brace of league championship medals with Manchester United and starred in two FA Cup final victories: one with United, the other with Manchester City. Together Leigh and Billy would form the backbone of Welsh sides for years to come, becoming firm friends in the process.

The game against Ireland gave Leigh the opportunity to show off his entire repertoire of tricks. Receiving the ball in the opening minute he advanced as far as the halfway line, bouncing it as he went, before sending a giant kick downfield towards the Irish goal, only returning to the safe haven of his own penalty area once he was sure the Welsh attack had broken up. Shortly before half-time he saved a shot from six yards out by trapping the ball between his knees. When the referee blew his whistle for the interval Leigh turned and bowed to the supporters behind his goal before running from the pitch to join the rest of the team. Few in the crowd of 6,000 had ever seen anything like it.

But it was to be one particular incident during the second half that really made people's heads turn. With Wales leading 1-0 thanks to a goal from Thomas David Parry, the visitors launched an attack down the right wing through Harry O'Reilly. Eager to nip any danger in the bud, Leigh sprinted from his goalmouth and deliberately bundled the Irishman into touch, knocking him unconscious in the process. Today such a challenge could well end up as a civil action in court. In 1900, while encapsulating the physical nature of the sport, it still proved to be the main talking point in the local taverns afterwards. Goalkeepers were meant to be the victims, not the aggressors, right? Leigh disagreed. If a centre forward could do that to a goalkeeper, then a goalkeeper was perfectly entitled to do something similar in return. The referee must have been thinking along the same lines as he didn't even award a free kick.

During the closing minutes Meredith added a second goal from the penalty spot and Leigh had made a winning start to his international career. Unfortunately Wales' final Home Nations game against England in Cardiff clashed with another cup tie for Aberystwyth Town who had advanced to the latter stages of three competitions – the Towyn Cup, the South Wales Cup and the prestigious Welsh Cup. With the club now reportedly covering Leigh's living as well as match expenses, there was only ever going to be one winner.

By the middle of April Town had already captured both the South Wales and Towyn Cups, defeating Rogerstone in the former by 1-0 after extra-time. Only one game now stood between them completing a unique treble. On 16 April over 3,000 people descended on Newtown in mid-Wales to watch Town take on the powerful Ruabon side Druids in the final of the Welsh Cup. Though Druids had lost several of their best players to English professional clubs during the 1890s, the result was expected to be close. It wasn't, and Town cruised to a comfortable 3-0 win. After the final whistle the crowd carried the victorious goalkeeper shoulder high from the field, even though it had been one of his quieter games.

Remarkably neither the *Western Mail*, the self-proclaimed national newspaper of Wales, nor the *South Wales Echo* saw fit to print the result of the 1900 Welsh Cup final let alone a match report. The one page of sport carried by the *Western Mail* the day after Aberystwyth Town's win was devoted entirely to rugby union and horse racing. Another decade would pass before the Welsh press finally woke up to the burgeoning interest in the round ball game, their coverage of international and major domestic club games finally doing justice to the thousands flocking to see the action.

With the 20th century less than four months old, Leigh already had three medals and a first international cap to his name. But he remained a big fish in a parochial Welsh pond. After 85 appearances for the side known as the 'Old black and green', it was time to move on.

3

Down to London

THE summer of 1900 was one of decisions for Leigh.
Having left Aberystwyth and returned to Holt to
spend time with his family, he now had to work out
what to do next with his life. Medicine remained his chosen
career path, the one that would eventually pay the bills,
but he also wanted to continue as an amateur footballer
playing the game at a decent level in exchange for expenses
only. Free to go wherever he pleased (his relationship
with Catherine Lewis was now over), Leigh scoured the
British Isles for a town or city where he would be able to
indulge both passions. Birmingham and Manchester were
ultimately rejected in favour of the traditional number
one destination for provincial twenty-somethings keen on
getting ahead in life and having a good time – London.

Come October Leigh packed his bags and caught
the train to London's Euston station, relatively near the
apartment he had arranged to rent in Hill Street, Mayfair,
from his second cousin Dr Robson Roose, a distinguished
physician. On Mondays to Fridays he cut his professional

teeth working as an assistant at King's College Hospital in Holborn, then as it is now a highly respected teaching centre (it would move to its present site south of the River Thames in 1913). Unable to secure a berth on that year's student intake for the Bachelor of Medicine degree because all the places had already been snapped up, he took every opportunity to watch the physicians, surgeons and research staff practising their work at close quarters. By doing so, Leigh hoped to get a better idea about what branch of medicine he might want to specialise in before applying again for a student place the following year.

Although the 1900/01 football season was already two months old, Leigh had little trouble finding a club in need of a goalkeeper. Ten years previously a group of friends belonging to Welsh regiments stationed in the English capital had formed the London Welsh Football Club. Besides playing football its aim was to 'honourably uphold the reputation of Wales in the Metropolis' in the same way that the Caledonians Football Club did for London-based Scotsmen. Open to amateur players of Welsh origin and descent, the club grew quickly and spawned several international players during the 1890s including winger John Rea and goalkeeper Sam Gillam. Leigh had heard all about London Welsh during September 1900 while playing as a stopgap for Druids, the side he helped defeat in the Welsh Cup final five months earlier. Several former Druids players had moved to London for work and joined the club, as much for the social side as the football. With no friends in London, he decided to do likewise.

It didn't take long for Leigh to realise that the quality of football played by London Welsh wasn't much better than that of Aberystwyth Town or Druids. However, simply being at the club did wonders for his profile. Within days of him signing, the Anglo-Welsh grapevine went into overdrive. Gates soared as Londoners with connections west of Offa's Dyke came to watch Leigh in action. They were soon joined by sports writers from the national newspapers, attracted by tales of the maverick Welshman with the unique goalkeeping style.

Leigh helped his cause by playing well and it came as little surprise when he was named in the Wales side to face Scotland at Wrexham on 2 March 1901. With Billy Meredith unavailable, Wales were expected to struggle against a team that had hit them for five the previous year. Leigh hadn't read the script and managed to deny the Scottish attack until 16 minutes from the end when he was finally beaten by a shot from the Glasgow Rangers midfielder John Robertson. The game finished 1-1 with Thomas David Parry scoring a late equaliser.

Having shipped 16 goals to Scotland in the previous three meetings between the countries the result was welcomed in the Principality as a victory, one secured by the safe hands of a goalkeeper winning only his second cap. With this morale booster under their belts, Wales travelled north two weeks later to take on England at Newcastle. Despite the return of Meredith, it wasn't even a contest. Leigh pulled off several outstanding saves but England still scored six without reply. A 1-0 victory over Ireland in Belfast five days later couldn't disguise the fact that Wales still had a long way to go before they could shake off their whipping boys tag.

For a goalkeeper there is one golden advantage of playing in a weak side – like it or not, you're going to get plenty of opportunities to show off your skills. Leigh saw an awful lot of action in all three of Wales' Home Nations games that year, which only enhanced his burgeoning reputation. Throughout what remained of the season he received telegrams from many of England's top clubs eager to acquire his services. Some went direct to his apartment, others arrived care of King's College Hospital. All wanted him to turn professional and sign a contract.

Despite being flattered by the attention, there was a problem. Turning professional would mean having to give up any plans for a career in medicine, and Leigh wasn't sure he was ready to do that. He had already enrolled on the degree course at King's due to begin that October, his heart now set on studying bacteriology (the study of minute organisms in living things). Besides, he didn't consider football to be a proper job. Fun, yes. But as a means of earning a living, no way.

Leigh's attitude would change later that summer with the arrival of yet another telegram, this one from Stoke City. Unable to compete financially with the vast majority of other clubs in the First Division of the Football League, Stoke were on the lookout for amateur players prepared to play for expenses only. Leigh replied, saying he would agree to join on two conditions – that he be allowed to continue living in London, and working at the hospital. Stoke not only agreed to both terms but also offered him an unlimited expenses account – first class train travel, the best hotels for overnight stays, plus certain 'extras' such as new suits, designer shoes and help with his rent. It was one hell of a gamble. Stoke were willing to pay whatever it took, hoping interest in the Welshman's arrival would translate into thousands more attending home games. It was also one that flew dangerously close to breaking FA laws regarding payments allowed to amateur players. Leigh may not have realised it, but he was now a professional in everything but name.

Scarcely able to believe his luck, Leigh told London Welsh that he wouldn't be able to turn out for them during the 1901/02 season. He also relinquished his place on the forthcoming degree course, intent on remaining a humble assistant at King's for the foreseeable future. On Saturday 12 October 1901, Leigh was officially registered as a Stoke City player.

≪-≫

Formed in 1863, Stoke had taken part in a mixture of friendly games and FA Cup ties for 25 years until invited by the Football Association to become one of the 12 founding members of the inaugural Football League. The League, which subsequently became the blueprint for every other competition of its kind around the world, involved teams playing each other both home and away over the course of a season with two points being awarded for a win and one for a draw (the current three points for a win system wasn't introduced until 1981). Stoke were little short of dreadful during the 1888/89 and 1889/90 campaigns, finishing bottom on both occasions.

With other clubs desperate to join City were voted out and replaced by ambitious Sunderland, only to be welcomed back in the following year when the League was expanded from 12 to 14 clubs.

Ten years later Stoke were still struggling finding themselves second from bottom ahead of Blackburn Rovers' visit to the Victoria Ground, City's pre-Britannia Stadium home, in what would be Leigh's debut. A series of poor performances had seen attendances fall as low as 3,000. On this occasion it would be almost three times that number, the publicity surrounding Leigh's arrival ensuring that as the clock ticked round to 3pm on Saturday 19 October 1901, the crowd were in a state of fever pitch.

Four minutes before kick-off Leigh emerged from the main stand and sprinted to the middle of the park. He bowed in turn to all four sides of the stadium, made his way towards the penalty area that Stoke had chosen to defend, and embarked on his now traditional pre-match ritual – walking from one side of the area to the other and back again, muttering under his breath. He also jumped into the air and swung for a few seconds on the crossbar. Nothing unusual about that today, but eccentric behaviour of the highest order in 1901. The crowd loved it. Before even kicking or catching a ball, Leigh had Stoke's supporters in the palm of his hand.

The game finished 2-2 with one journalist moved to report that 'Roose certainly is a class custodian'. Despite not being at fault for either of Blackburn's goals Leigh was critical of his own performance, remarking afterwards that "perhaps the sense of occasion had somewhat affected my early concentration." Although a family engagement prevented Leigh from playing the following week at Everton, he was back for the visit of top-of-the-table Sunderland at the beginning of November. The visitors dominated the opening 20 minutes but failed to score with Leigh saving two shots from close range. Inspired by some stout defending Stoke fought their way back into the game, eventually cruising to a comfortable 3-0 win. Two days later they defeated Wolverhampton Wanderers by the same score at the Victoria Ground. Gradually, City began to climb away from the foot of the table.

Stoke's improvement wasn't solely down to Leigh. Among the other amateurs attracted by the club's generous expenses offer were accountant/inside forward Leonard

Hales and defender Sam Ashworth, an architect who went on to build schools across Stoke-on-Trent for the local education authority. Alongside Ashworth at the centre of defence stood the professional Tom Holford, all 5ft 5ins of him. Born in nearby Hanley and weighing just 9st, Holford made up for his diminutive frame by playing an aggressive no-nonsense game, giving rise to the nickname 'Dirty Tommy'. Then there was centre forward Mart Watkins, an international colleague of Leigh's, born and raised on a farm in mid-Wales. An unselfish player, popular with his teammates and supporters, Mart's 16-goal haul between August 1901 and April 1902 would prove crucial in Stoke's battle to avoid relegation.

Yet with his inventive play and oddball ways, it was Leigh who more often than not grabbed the headlines. As the season progressed so his behaviour both on and off the pitch grew more outrageous. During games he began talking with the crowds assembled behind his goal, encouraging them to applaud good play but also cracking jokes, often regarding mistakes made by opposing players. While this proved popular with spectators at the Victoria Ground it didn't always go down well when Stoke played away from home. In one match at Bramall Lane he was struck on the back of the head by a coin after loudly remarking that Sheffield United "would have to do considerably better than that" if they were going to beat him.

In another fixture at Manchester City Leigh faked nerves while an opponent shaped up to take a penalty by wobbling his knees maniacally, something Liverpool goalkeeper Bruce Grobbelaar would also famously use to his advantage 82 years later in a European Cup final against the Italian side AS Roma. After saving the kick Leigh turned to the Manchester supporters behind the goal and with a broad grin on his face raised his arms in triumph, only to have an apple thrown at him by an irate spectator.

As if that wasn't enough there was also his carefully stage-managed arrivals at the Victoria Ground prior to games. Having caught a morning train from London Euston to Stoke, Leigh would usually arrange for a hansom cab to meet him at the station. Taking the reins himself he would then drive at speed through the city's streets, pulling up outside the stadium to be mobbed by crowds arriving for the game. Throughout its journey the cab would be chased by dozens of young supporters trying to keep up with their hero.

While Leigh divided opinion with his on-field pranks, occasionally attracting accusations of bad sportsmanship, nobody doubted his incredible ability. He played with the same calmness and authority in the First Division (now the Premier League) as he had displayed in friendly games for London Welsh. The renowned football writer Ivan Sharpe said the first time he watched Leigh, he presumed he was playing at either left or right back rather than in goal. 'Everything he did was magical', Sharpe later wrote. 'He was a law unto himself'.

Though one misguided journalist from *The Times* referred to his constant coming out of goal as 'a weakness', the tactic was certainly paying dividends for Stoke. Centre forwards began talking about the hypnotic effect Leigh seemed to have as they advanced towards the penalty area, almost daring them to bring the ball any closer. Word of his bravery and willingness to charge down opponents also began to spread. In 1905, Leigh himself wrote, 'A goalkeeper should take in the position at once and at a glance and, if deemed necessary, come out of his goal immediately. He must be regardless of his personal consequences and, if necessary, go head first into a pack into which many men would hesitate to insert a foot, and take the consequent gruelling like a Spartan. I am convinced that the reason why goalkeepers don't come out of their goal more often is their regard for personal consequences. If a forward has to be met and charged down, do not hesitate to charge with all your might!'

On several occasions during Leigh's debut season in the First Division journalists drew comparisons between the goalkeeper and a prize fighter, glowering down at poleaxed centre forwards the way a boxer might after flooring an opponent. In reality the gladiator-style posturing was all part of an elaborate act. Leigh liked playing to the crowds and tried giving them the kind of entertainment he would want to see if he were a spectator. Football was important, but he never lost sight of the fact it was just a game. "A pinch of salt was a good condiment but if they took a spoonful it became nauseating," he told one reporter from the *Oswestry Advertiser*. "Sport should be regarded as the salt of life, not as the main object and purpose of a man's career."

By the beginning of 1902 Stoke had managed to put some distance between themselves and the group of other clubs struggling to avoid relegation from the First Division. On the morning of Saturday 4 January the team travelled to Liverpool for a league fixture, meeting in a hotel near Lime Street railway station for a pre-match meal and to talk tactics. Whatever plans they came up with went out of the window just 10 minutes into the game when Leigh, without any warning, suddenly ran from the field and began vomiting in the dressing room. Within 20 minutes he had been joined by the equally ill Sam Ashworth who warned one of Stoke's directors, Dr Moody, that several other players were also feeling unwell.

At half-time Moody examined the team individually and declared that four of them – Leigh, Ashworth, Mart

Watkins and centre forward Frank Whitehouse – were unfit to continue. The only people other than Moody in the Stoke party who appeared unaffected were the club's two trainers. The doctor quickly deduced that they were the ones who hadn't had plaice for lunch. "The dressing room resembled the cabin of a cross-Channel steamer in bad weather, and smelt like it.....only more so," Moody told journalists afterwards, adding that Leigh's pulse rate when he left the field had risen to 148 beats per minute (the normal resting rate for a healthy adult is between 60 and 100 beats per minute).

Stoke took the field for the second half with just seven players, all of them fighting the effects of food poisoning. They soon began conceding goals, going on to lose 7-0 despite the gallant reappearance of both Watkins and Whitehouse. As if to prove that seven definitely wasn't a lucky number City went on to lose their next seven games, plunging back towards the foot of the table in the process.

Four weeks after the Liverpool fiasco Stoke's season took another turn for the worse when Bristol Rovers lodged an official protest with the Football Association regarding Leigh's appearance against them in an FA Cup tie. Rovers insisted that the Welsh international had already played in a qualifying round of the cup that season for London Welsh against the wonderfully named Crouch End Vampires, and was therefore barred from appearing for another club. Stoke were livid. Leigh's outstanding performance against the west country side had been crucial to City's 1-0 victory. What's more, the club had given Rovers a list of their team five days before the game and no objections were received. The whole thing smacked of sour grapes.

It was London Welsh who sprang to the defence of their former goalkeeper. They admitted that although Leigh's name had appeared in the official programme for the Crouch End game, it had been an administrative mistake. The explanation was accepted by the Football Association and Bristol Rovers, but only after a bitter war of words had been played out between the two clubs on the pages of the national newspapers.

Leigh did his best to remain focused by simply ignoring the whole messy business which dragged on until early April 1902. Work commitments at King's meant that during February and March he had been forced to pull out of three Saturday games, two for Stoke and one for Wales against Ireland. When he was available to play, Leigh wanted to make sure he was at least in the right frame of mind to do so. With the exception of a 5-1 thrashing at the hands of Scotland in Greenock on 15 March, when by all accounts every Welsh player had a stinker, his ploy seemed to work. He even managed to keep a clean sheet against England in a 0-0 draw at Wrexham, the first Welsh goalkeeper to do so since 1881 – a run of 20 consecutive games.

Stoke's seven match losing streak meant that come the beginning of April they were still in danger of being relegated. Again, Leigh was forced to miss the first game of the month, a 2-1 home defeat to Sheffield United, because of work commitments. Despite his growing stature in the game, plus the thrill of playing First Division football, Leigh knew that if he was ever going to make it in medicine then he couldn't afford to upset the hierarchy at King's. After all, the destiny of his post-football career lay in their hands. Stoke just had to bite the bullet if their first-choice goalkeeper, playing without a contract and for expenses only, had to work the occasional Saturday.

On Saturday 7 April Leigh returned for the visit of Bolton Wanderers to the Victoria Ground. Defeat would in all likelihood spell relegation. The early signs didn't look good. Bolton dominated much of the first half but couldn't find a way past Stoke's goalkeeper who had done his best to whip the home crowd into a frenzy from the moment he drew up in his hansom cab. Slowly City began to turn the screw and, much as they had done against Sunderland back in November, ended up with a comfortable win, this time by 4-0. The following week Stoke confirmed their place in the First Division for another season by seeing off Grimsby Town 2-0.

With their limited financial clout, Stoke celebrated survival as if they had won the title. On the Wednesday evening after the Grimsby game the club threw a banquet for which Leigh travelled up especially from London. At some point during the festivities he was cornered by Horace Austerberry, Stoke City's secretary and team manager, who asked if he would consider playing for another season. Leigh didn't need much persuading. Within the space of seven months at the Victoria Ground his star had risen to the point where he was now one of the most recognisable sportsmen in Britain. He enjoyed the adulation. On returning to London the following day he once again withdrew from his degree course, which was scheduled to begin in October 1902, intent on remaining an assistant at King's for another year.

In a round-up of the 1901/02 First Division season in the *Athletic News*, the national weekly paper dedicated exclusively to sport, journalist James Catton went as far as describing Leigh as 'the Prince of Goalkeepers'. It was a title that had been loosely bestowed before most notably on Sunderland's Teddy Doig. This time around it seemed to stick. From the summer of 1902, there would be only one Prince.

4

Ten Cads and a Goalkeeper

LONDON life was growing ever more comfortable for Leigh Richmond Roose. He dressed in the finest clothes, attended the best West End shows, ate at the cream of the capital's restaurants, drank at the most exclusive gentlemen's clubs. And as he was earning only an average wage at King's College Hospital, it was Stoke City who more often than not picked up the tab. Being a famous sportsman he often got away without paying at all. Establishments wanted to be associated with Leigh. If that meant providing free tickets, meals or drinks, then so be it.

Most weekday evenings, usually after work and before hitting the town, Leigh would go running in Regent's Park to maintain his fitness levels. With so many amateur players on Stoke's books, finding the time to train together was a near impossibility. Occasionally before big games the team would try and set aside part of the previous day to rehearse a few moves. But the norm was to discuss tactics over lunch two or three hours before kick-off.

An added bonus was the arrival in London of his sister, Helena. The two had always been close growing up in Holt with Helena making regular trips to Aberystwyth to visit Leigh during his university days. Now she had met a young South Wales Borderer by the name of John Jenkins, a keen sportsman who by coincidence played rugby for London Welsh and would go on to win one Welsh cap against South Africa in 1906. The pair married and bought a house in Mount View Road, Crouch End, which Leigh came to use as a second home when tired of the confines of his Mayfair pad.

If one word were to sum up Stoke's form throughout Leigh's second season at the club, it would be inconsistent. Win followed defeat followed win followed defeat, with the odd draw thrown in for good measure. A 5-0 opening day reverse at Newcastle became a 5-0 victory in the return fixture at the Victoria Ground four months later. Predictably unpredictable, they were at least winning far more games than they had the previous season.

Besides Leigh, Maurice Austerberry had successfully talked the whole of the team into committing themselves to the club for another year. As a unit they were wiser having learned from the mistakes that had so nearly cost Stoke their First Division status last time around. But Leigh remained City's prized asset. If anything he was on even better form, managing to shed half a stone in weight over the summer to become leaner and quicker. Many a centre forward, latching on to a through pass 40 yards or more from goal, found the ball whipped off his toes by one of Leigh's boots before they knew what was happening. Those that did manage to advance any distance often lost their cool, lashing shots into the crowd from long range rather than risk colliding with the menacing frame of the onrushing Welshman. The accuracy of his notoriously long kicks and throws improved while he also began punching the ball more as a way of keeping the game flowing. When safe to do so he would frequently dribble it out of the penalty area with his feet, eyes scanning the field for a teammate to pass to – anything to keep the opposition guessing about which way he planned to launch an attack.

'Players with the intelligence to devise a new move or system, and application to carry it out, will go far', Leigh wrote in 1905, adding that a goalkeeper 'need not set out to keep goal on the usual stereotype lines. He is at liberty to cultivate originality and, more often than not, if he has a variety of methods in his clearance and means of getting rid of the ball, he will confound and puzzle the attacking forwards. Let a goalkeeper be successful in his clearances, and great will be his triumph. Let him fail, and oblivion will be his portion'.

If there was a criticism, it was that Leigh's ability to confound and puzzle extended to players on his own side who sometimes had no idea what he was planning on doing next. Though mistakes did happen (against Sheffield Wednesday he lost possession while dribbling the ball out of his area, leaving a grateful centre forward with an empty net to aim at) they were so rare that his teammates tended to let them pass without comment. As Sam Ashworth commented, "He plays like no other custodian in the land dares to play. That's why he is the man that he is."

Leigh's only other minor flaw at this stage in his career (besides overstepping the mark with the odd joke to the crowd) was his bizarre refusal to wear a clean kit for each league match. Exactly why, nobody knew. As the *Cricket &*

Football Field magazine put it, 'Roose is one of the cleanest custodians we have, but he apparently is a trifle superstitious about his football garments for he seldom seems to trouble the charwoman with them'. When playing for Wales or in important cup ties for Stoke, he would often wear his old black and green Aberystwyth Town shirt beneath his jersey, an item of kit he had apparently refused to wash since Town's victorious Welsh Cup final win over Druids. He believed it would bring him good luck.

As with any sporting side boasting an outstanding individual talent, Stoke did attract taunts from opposition fans and some members of the press that they were little more than a one man team. Strangely the club did little to counter such jibes. Quite the opposite. Towards the end of February 1903 Leigh damaged ligaments in his left knee during an away match against Nottingham Forest. Despite being in pain he managed to play on and keep a clean sheet in a 0-0 draw. The following week he underwent surgery in Manchester to repair the damage, intending to be ready for Stoke's FA Cup third round tie at Derby County on 7 March. On the day of the game he discharged himself from hospital but could barely walk, forcing his withdrawal from the team. Stoke lost 3-1, Horace Austerberry saying afterwards that Leigh's absence meant "they were beaten before they made their bow."

Deep down Leigh knew that if the injury was going to mend properly, then it needed at least four months' complete rest from football. On the advice of doctors in Manchester and at King's he informed both Stoke and the Football Association of Wales that he would be unable to play for the rest of the season, ruling himself out of eight league games and three Home Nations fixtures. His place in the Welsh side went to Bob Evans who performed well but wasn't able to prevent a clean sweep of defeats to England (1-2), Scotland (0-1) and Ireland (0-2). On the other hand Stoke, with Leigh's understudy Thomas Wilkes in goal, embarked on an impressive run which saw them rise from mid-table to the fringes of the race for the First Division title, dispelling the one man team myth for good. A 2-0 defeat to Aston Villa on 18 April derailed any hopes the club had of winning the league for the first time, and they ended up finishing fifth – still, in the words of the *Athletic News*, a 'proud position'.

Despite Wilkes' fine end-of-season form Leigh was told the goalkeeper's jersey was his for the following campaign, providing he was fit and wanted to continue playing for Stoke. As in 1901 and 1902, Leigh had put his name down to start the Bachelor of Medicine degree course at King's in October 1903. He withdrew yet again, happy to continue with his double life as star footballer and hospital assistant for another year. Full-time study would also have meant a dip in living standards with nobody around to bankroll his London lifestyle. As an attractive, single, 25-year-old man about town with an image to maintain, he needed Stoke City as much as the club required him.

That summer, as Leigh put his knee through its paces by running around Regent's Park, Stoke went to work redeveloping the Victoria Ground aiming to make it one of the finest sporting arenas in the country. This, the club's directors believed, would lead to two things – more people coming to watch Stoke play, which in turn would generate the extra revenue required to bring in better players. Their plan was, however, fatally flawed. To begin with City had to borrow money to fund the redevelopment work, putting a club that was already perilously close to the breadline into debt. In addition, people were only going to pay to watch a successful side, or at least one that won more games than it lost.

During the 1903/04 season Stoke lost considerably more games than they won. Although the side had looked sharp in their summer warm-up matches too many players performed well below par once the week-to-week treadmill of the league programme got under way. Thankfully for City, Leigh wasn't one of them. With his defenders low on confidence virtually every game became a duel between him and the opposition's forwards. Initially Leigh loved it. It gave him more work to do and a platform on which to show off. But as morale throughout the team dipped, so doing the round trip from London to Stoke (or often further afield for away games) started becoming something of a bind.

At the beginning of 1904 City asked Leigh to make significant reductions in his expenses claims. Instead of climbing well above 10,000 for each home game, attendances at the improved Victoria Ground were still hanging around the 6,000 mark or less in the wake of a bad defeat. Cutbacks were the order of the day throughout the club. Travel and accommodation fees would be fine, together with the occasional clothing allowance, but everything else would have to go including the claims for food and drink, furniture for his apartment and hansom cabs. Leigh believed he was playing to the best of his ability and that Stoke had no right to go back on their original offer of an unlimited expense account, made in 1901. He expressed his feelings to Horace Austerberry but was told there was simply no alternative if he wanted to carry on playing for the club.

On 28 March 1904 Stoke lost 3-0 away to relegation rivals West Bromwich Albion. They were now second from bottom of the First Division and appeared doomed. The following Saturday ahead of their final away game of the season at Everton the players met in a Liverpool hotel for lunch, during which a few home truths were aired. Horace Austerberry had his say, spelling out in no uncertain terms that relegation would mean the vast majority of them looking for new clubs. If intended as a call to arms, it worked. Stoke won 1-0 and other results went their way. Liverpool and West Bromwich Albion would be the two sides making the drop.

Knowing they were already safe, City drew 1-1 at home against Derby County on the final day of the season. The campaign ended on a sour note for Leigh. Running out of his penalty area in an attempt to kick the ball clear, he mistimed the bounce completely and fell over allowing County's England international Steve Bloomer to shoot into an unguarded net. Immediately after the game Leigh stunned the club by announcing that he was quitting football altogether to concentrate on his medical career. His teammates, wary of the Welshman's fondness for practical jokes, thought he was kidding. City's directors dismissed it as nothing more than a bad case of the blues brought on by his mistake. In time, he would surely reconsider. But Leigh was serious. His first two years at Stoke had been an adventure beyond his wildest dreams. The third, tainted by near relegation and the row over his expenses, had at times been miserable. Privately, he also believed that his form had dipped towards the end of the season as demonstrated by the sloppy goal conceded against Derby County. If he wasn't at his best, then he didn't want to play. Anyway, by his own admission there were more important things to life than football.

That evening, without even saying a proper farewell to the fans who had elevated him to hero status, he caught a train from Stoke back to London intending never to play league football again.

<< →>

Today you barely have to lift a finger to receive the latest sports news. It's all around us – radio stations, TV channels, apps, betting websites, daily newspaper supplements dedicated entirely to sport, all trying to outdo each other with the latest gossip, odds and interviews. In 1904 things were slightly different. Short of actually being there, the only way of finding out whether Liverpool had won at Sunderland or how Surrey were doing at The Oval was by reading a newspaper, one carrying perhaps two pages of sport rather than the 20-plus of recent times. The exception to the rule was the *Athletic News* with anything up to a dozen pages, but that only appeared once a week on Mondays.

In such an era it's hardly surprising that news of Leigh's premature retirement took some time to filter out. As a rule the *Athletic News* marked the end of every football season by virtually ignoring the game for the next four months, concentrating almost entirely on cricket instead. At some point during the summer both Stoke City and the Football Association of Wales received letters from Leigh officially informing them of his decision. But it wasn't until August 1904 when the *News* ran its annual club-by-club guide to the forthcoming First Division season that his retirement was confirmed publicly.

The general reaction within the game, the media and among supporters was one of astonishment. Almost everyone knew Leigh had some kind of interest in medicine. A handful of journalists were aware that he planned on eventually returning to college with a view to becoming a doctor. But to retire aged just 26, less than three years after making his First Division debut, seemed ludicrous. So what if he'd made a couple of glaring errors towards the end of the previous season? All goalkeepers occasionally make mistakes, even the best in the land, which in 1904 Leigh undoubtedly was.

Several clubs did their best to get him to change his mind including Liverpool and Woolwich Arsenal. All received polite 'thanks but no thanks' replies. In October, having banked enough savings to take him through the lion's share of his three-year course, he returned to full-time education. The Bachelor of Medicine degree course would give him a solid grounding in all forms of medicine from practical toxicology to pathological anatomy. Come the end of 1907 Leigh would be free to concentrate on his specialised area of bacteriology either at King's or quite possibly abroad (besides travelling to Belfast with the Welsh team, he had yet to set foot outside the British mainland).

At least that was the plan. Leigh enjoyed his lectures and the practical side of the course, especially dealing directly with patients. His sporting background made him the centre of attention among fellow male scholars (King's didn't start admitting women as students until 1918), always among the first on the guest list for any parties or gatherings. However, as the weeks rolled by, the truth began to hit home – he missed football. Never was this sense of loss more acutely felt than on Saturday afternoons. Stuck in London with no lectures to attend and little money to enjoy himself, he became increasingly bored and frustrated. Reading the match reports in Monday's papers only added to his growing sense of restlessness.

By November, Leigh had made his mind up that he wanted to resume playing, preferably in the First Division.

It was just a matter of finding the right club, one that would accept him as a London-based amateur intent on remaining a student from Monday to Friday, something that would occasionally make him unavailable for midweek games. He didn't have to wait long. On Thursday 17 November a delegation from Everton Football Club visited Leigh during a break in lectures at King's to ask a favour. Bill Scott, their first-choice goalkeeper, had injured a shoulder and was expected to be out for up to three weeks. His understudy, George Kitchen, had influenza leaving Everton with nobody to fill the gap between the posts that coming Saturday against Sunderland. The club had made Leigh its number one target as a replacement, but with little more than 48 hours until kick-off couldn't afford to wait long for a decision.

There was little doubt in Leigh's mind that Everton were the right club for him, one of the most famous in the land with a team packed full of internationals. They were so right that he almost declined their offer. His only appearance in goal since April had been for Oxford City as a favour for a friend who played at the club. Desperately short of match practice, Leigh didn't want to let Everton – or perhaps more importantly himself – down. After an hour of discussions held at a pub in Holborn, he finally agreed not only to play against Sunderland but until Scott was fit enough to return to the side. Everton had their man.

On the Saturday morning Leigh made his way to Euston and caught an early express for Liverpool. He was welcomed at the city's Lime Street station by a small crowd, alerted to his impending arrival by a story in that day's *Liverpool Echo*, and two club officials who accompanied him to Everton's Goodison Park ground. Once there he met his new teammates for the first time as allies, including Scott.

"He is one of the finest, if not the finest, goalkeepers in the land," the injured player told waiting journalists. "At least I know my colleagues are in the best of hands. Leigh Richmond Roose won't let them down."

As it turned out, Leigh Richmond Roose did let them down. Five minutes before half-time he failed to catch a cross which, according to the *Athletic News*, Leigh would 'normally have saved 19 times out of 20' allowing Sunderland's Arthur Bridgett to score what proved to be the only goal of the game. The error came in front of a full house at Goodison including around 60 people who had travelled up especially for the occasion from Holt. On the final whistle Bridgett, who had played alongside Leigh for two years at Stoke City, walked from the field with a sympathetic arm draped across his former teammate's shoulders. It was anything but the dream debut he had wished for.

With Scott and Kitchen still unavailable, Everton had no alternative but to select Leigh again for their following game at home to Derby County a fortnight later. Grateful to be given an opportunity to make amends, he spent at least a quarter of an hour before kick-off walking around the outside of the pitch shaking hands with supporters and apologising for his error against Sunderland. As a public relations exercise, it was a masterstroke. Leigh went on to keep a clean sheet in a 0-0 draw, bowing and saluting to the crowd after several saves. His prodigious kicks, throws and punches drew gasps and applause from around the ground. During an injury-enforced stoppage in the second half he even pulled himself up onto the crossbar and sat on the wooden beam until play resumed. Cue widespread laughter.

The following Saturday it was Stoke City's turn to visit Goodison. If Leigh's former side harboured any bitterness over his decision to resume playing so soon after quitting the club, they hid it well. Maurice Austerberry had even sent a telegram on the day of the Sunderland game wishing him good luck. For the first time in several weeks Everton hit top gear and ran out 4-1 winners. In the closing minutes Stoke were awarded a penalty following a foul by the England international forward Jimmy Settle on Tom Holford. City's Frank Whitehead stepped forward to take the kick, drilling his shot hard and low to the goalkeeper's left side. Leigh parried it with one hand, then fell on the loose ball before Whitehead had time to react to the rebound. If there were any doubts about whether he could still cut it at the highest level after so many months away from the game, then they were dispelled at that moment.

The Stoke game proved to be a huge turning point in Everton's season. Languishing in mid-table at the start of play, the club won 12 and drew three of their next 16 league games. Come the end of January 1905 they were top of the pile. Leigh's outstanding form meant he remained the first-choice goalkeeper even after Scott had recovered from his shoulder injury. But the galaxy of top players in front of him made his job as the last line of defence all the easier. Men like half back Harry Makepeace, an England international at both football and cricket who hit 117 and 54 runs against Australia in Melbourne during the fourth Test of the 1920/21 tour; pint-sized yet stylish winger Harold Hardman who like Leigh insisted on remaining an amateur player; centre forward Alex Young whose winning goal in the 1906 FA Cup final was described by one journalist as having a similar effect on the blue half of Liverpool as that of an earthquake on San Francisco the previous week; and Settle, who Evertonians claimed could make a racehorse blush with his pace.

As the victories began to stack up in both the league and the FA Cup, so a common consensus steadily grew among supporters and the media that Everton were somehow destined to achieve the 'double' that season. Dedicated to attractive, attacking football, they won new friends wherever they played with Leigh – thanks to a combination of skill and showmanship – donning the role of team talisman. On 18 February they travelled to Stoke's Victoria Ground for an FA Cup second round game (the equivalent of today's fourth round for Premier League and Championship clubs). Although no official attendance was given for Leigh's return to the club he had served for three years, estimates varied at between 14,000 and 16,000, well over twice the usual figure. Unsure whether they were there to welcome or lynch him, Leigh decided not to wave or bow to the crowd but to simply sprint onto the pitch and go through his traditional pre-match ritual of pacing from one side of the penalty area to the other and back.

He need not have worried. The ovation he received was loud and heartfelt. Several spectators went the extra mile by running on to the field prior to kick-off to shake hands with their former hero.

Everton completely overpowered their opponents that day, winning 4-0 with Makepeace and Settle among the goalscorers. Such was the high standard of their play that during the second half many of Everton's fluent moves were applauded by the home supporters. It was much the same story in the next round of the FA Cup, Settle grabbing a hat-trick as Southampton were also defeated 4-0.

In the semi-finals Everton were paired with Aston Villa. The tie was fixed for 25 March to be played at a neutral venue – none other than the Victoria Ground. If anything Leigh received an even better reception than he had the previous month, several thousand Stoke City diehards sacrificing a spare Saturday afternoon to cheer him on. But the goodwill of the north Staffordshire people wasn't enough to see Everton through to their third FA Cup final. Despite dominating play the game finished all square at 1-1. Both teams would have to do it all over again in four days' time at the City Ground in Nottingham.

Before then Leigh had the small matter of a Welsh international match against England in Liverpool to think about. On returning to the game the previous November he had taken the unusual step of writing to the Football Association of Wales asking to be considered for the forthcoming Home Nations games of 1905. Though the FAW had other goalkeepers at their disposal, a fit Leigh Richmond Roose was always going to be first choice. Along with Billy Meredith, he remained Wales' most valuable player. Without either man, the Principality stood very little chance of winning a first Home Nations Championship. Having proved he was back to his best form with Everton, Leigh went straight into the Welsh team to face Scotland in Wrexham on 6 March.

In the event Leigh's eighth international cap proved to be one of his quietest, Wales coasting to a comfortable 3-1 win against disappointing opponents. England in Liverpool would be a different proposition, even with a full strength Welsh side plus the backing of around 2,000 supporters making the short trip from across the border. For Leigh the game took on an added significance following the decision by the Football Association of Wales to name him as captain, something he would look back on as one of the highlights of his career. "To play for one's country is an honour, no matter how many times one is selected to appear," he told football writer Ivan Sharpe. "To captain one's country is however the honour of honours, generating the kind of pride within a man that is difficult to define in words."

And so just 48 hours after appearing in an FA Cup semi-final Leigh went to work against England's forwards, sporting as ever that unwashed black and green Aberystwyth Town shirt beneath his Welsh jersey. The first half finished goalless with Wales, if anything, having the edge. But the second period was a different story, the outstanding Vivian Woodward of Tottenham Hotspur scoring twice as England ran out 3-1 winners (Woodward still holds the English record for scoring the most goals in a single international, hitting eight versus France in Paris in 1908). At the final whistle the Welsh goalkeeper and the England forward exchanged jerseys in a gesture of mutual respect.

Two days later Everton went head to head with Aston Villa again for the right to play Newcastle United in the FA Cup final at Crystal Palace. In one of their poorest performances for months they lost 2-1, only Everton's second defeat since Leigh's debut for them against Sunderland back in November 1904. The dream of the double was over. Unfortunately the hangover from the Villa game immediately started affecting their league form. With six games left to play Everton were top of the First Division, four points clear of their nearest rivals Newcastle United. The first three games – against Woolwich Arsenal, Stoke and Small Heath (who would later morph into Birmingham City) – produced five fortunate points from a trio of below par performances. That left three away matches within the space of just four days over the 1905 Easter weekend – at Manchester City, Woolwich Arsenal and Nottingham Forest. Two wins would be enough for The Toffees, as they were by now known, to clinch the First Division title for a second time.

Yet fate was by now beginning to conspire against Everton. Thirty-four league games a season plus six FA Cup ties might not seem especially taxing by today's standards. However, the extremely physical nature of the sport in Edwardian Britain, not to mention the fact that most of Everton's players had also played in the Home Nations internationals for their respective countries, meant there were a lot of extremely tired and bruised limbs in the side. Throw in the additional time it took to travel to away games in 1905, often sat in uncomfortable and overcrowded railway carriages, and you can see why attempting to play three over a 72-hour period spelled big trouble.

Then there was the added controversy over how the fixture pile-up had come about in the first place. The Woolwich Arsenal game had originally been scheduled for Saturday 26 November 1904. With just 13 minutes remaining and Everton leading 3-1, the referee abandoned the match due to the foggy conditions even though both teams were willing to play on. Rather than let the result stand, the FA ordered a replay. Quite why Everton agreed to the rearranged date of Saturday 22 April is a mystery. One can only assume that at the end of November, with the club lying in ninth place, winning the title was the last thing on anyone's mind.

On Good Friday morning the Everton team, minus Leigh (who travelled up from London separately), made the short train trip to Manchester. That afternoon they put in arguably their worst performance of the season, losing 2-0 to a Billy Meredith-inspired City side. By 10.45pm they were on another train bound for London, arriving bleary eyed in the capital a little over five hours later. Several members of the team then managed to grab a few hours' sleep at Leigh's apartment in Mayfair before heading across the city to the Manor Ground in Plumstead, Woolwich Arsenal's home from 1893 to 1913 prior to moving to Highbury. Unsurprisingly given their chaotic pre-match preparation, Everton duly lost 2-1.

Immediately afterwards, with their title dream in tatters, Leigh confronted manager William C Cuff regarding the wisdom of playing both games in such a short time frame with so much at stake. Cuff's reply went something along the following lines – if Leigh was so concerned about the fixture pile-up, then why had he dared ask permission to be excused from Everton's home game against Stoke two weeks earlier in order to play in a Home Nations international for Wales against Ireland in Belfast?

Cuff had a point. Upset over what he regarded as a challenge to his authority, he told Leigh that Bill Scott would play in Everton's final game of the season at Nottingham Forest on Easter Monday instead of him. Furious at having been dropped for the first time in his career (and for simply airing a point of view rather than poor form), Leigh refused to join his teammates on the train journey north, preferring to remain in London. Despite a combination of fatigue and dressing room unrest Everton somehow managed to win the game 2-0, but the result proved meaningless. Newcastle United's 3-0 victory at Middlesbrough meant they were crowned champions, The Toffees having to settle for second place.

Leigh would come to regret his fit of pique. Once the red mist had cleared, he wrote a letter to Cuff apologising for his behaviour and thanking Everton for giving him the opportunity to prove himself once again as a top class goalkeeper. He received no reply. After just five months and 24 appearances, Leigh's days as an Evertonian seemed numbered.

Sure enough, football's bush telegraph immediately sprang into action fuelled by a story printed in the Monday 1 May edition of the *Athletic News* containing details of the breakdown in relations between Cuff and his first-choice goalkeeper. Never one to miss a golden opportunity, Horace Austerberry immediately fired off a speculative telegram asking Leigh if he would consider returning to Stoke City. He didn't have to wait long for an answer, delivered by way of another telegram dated Wednesday 3 May containing just two words – 'Glad to'.

On paper it looked like a sensible marriage. Besides needing a new club, Leigh still enjoyed an excellent relationship with Stoke's supporters, as demonstrated by the reception afforded him on his two returns to the Potteries with Everton in the FA Cup. In turn, Stoke remained in the market for the best amateur players. Attendances for home games had continued to fall since Leigh's departure 12 months previously and there were high hopes that his return could help arrest or even reverse the decline, generating extra revenue.

And so on Saturday 2 September 1905 Leigh made his second debut for Stoke City. To the club's delight he not only kept a clean sheet against Notts County but also managed to multiply the previous home attendance of 4,000 three times over. Those present were treated to the full Leigh Richmond Roose bag of tricks – the infamous sorties to the halfway line, bone crunching tackles on advancing centre forwards, the cracking of jokes with people in the crowd – and they loved it. So too did the many journalists assigned to cover the game. 'I can pay the Welsh international no greater compliment than to say he is an even greater goalkeeper now than he was when he formerly wore the colours of Stoke', wrote the correspondent from the *Athletic*

News. 'In my opinion there is not his equal for smartness in getting down to a low shot apparently well out of reach'.

By the middle of November, with Stoke City third in the First Division, Leigh's star had risen to new heights. When the *Daily Mail* published its 'World XI' to challenge another planet at football, he was the undisputed choice for the goalkeeper's jersey. Journalists from newspapers throughout the land wrote requesting interviews, enticed by the story of the medical student fast becoming one of the most famous sportsmen of his time. The vast majority were granted on one condition – that the interview take place over lunch at Scott's seafood restaurant in London's Piccadilly, with the newspaper of course footing the bill.

One reporter from the *Bristol Times* wrote:

> 'Few men exhibit their personality so vividly in their play as L R Roose. You cannot spend five minutes in his company without being impressed by his vivacity, his boldness, his knowledge of men and things – a clever man undoubtedly, but entirely unrestrained in word or action. He rarely stands listlessly by the goalpost even when the ball is at the other end of the enclosure, but is ever following the play keenly and closely. Directly his charge is threatened, he is on the move. He thinks nothing of dashing out 10 or 15 yards, even when his backs have as good a chance of clearing as he makes for himself. He will also rush along the touchline, field the ball and get in a kick too, to keep the game going briskly. Equally daring and unorthodox are his methods of dealing with strong shots. He is not a model custodian by all means. He would not be L R Roose if he was'.

Other newspapers and magazines moved quickly to exploit Leigh's intellect and knowledge of the game by asking him to write about his experiences playing in goal, making him the first footballer in the UK (and possibly even the world) to produce regular columns. These became required reading for supporters of all clubs, eager to hear the opinions of an educated man on what remained a working class sport. They also provided Leigh with yet another source of income to support his studies and bachelor lifestyle.

More than a century later it's easy to dismiss much of Leigh's writing as little more than an exercise in stating the obvious ('The fairest judgement of a man is by the standard of his work, and the best goalkeeper is the one who makes the fewest mistakes' – the *Book of Football* magazine, 1906). Yet at the time his views represented a fresh take on a sport still in its relative infancy.

Some remain as valid today as they did during the early years of the 20th century. For example, from *The Times*, 1906:

> 'A goalkeeper and his methods of defence are the result of the physical makeup of the individual. He should stand about six foot and no nonsense. Size gives one the impression of strength and safety and enables a goalkeeper to deal with high and wide shots with comparative ease, where a smaller or shorter man would be handicapped. On the other hand, a tall and ponderous goalkeeper is at a disadvantage with the smaller and more agile rival when required to get down to swift ground or low shots. To the agility of youth should be coupled the sagacity of veterancy'.

From the *Daily Mail*, 1906:

> 'Goalkeeping is not only a physical exercise but a moral discipline when looked upon in its true light and from a right and proper standpoint. It develops courage, perseverance, endurance and other qualities which fit one for fighting the battle of life. It is an education of body and mind'.

If there was one minor criticism, it was Leigh's erudite style of writing even by Edwardian standards. "As a child, I remember seeing people on the tube screwing up their faces in amazement as they read his articles in the *Football Evening News*," recalled Dick Jenkins, Leigh's nephew, in 2000. "My mother used to nudge me and point them out. Sometimes it was difficult to tell whether they were amazed at what they were reading or couldn't understand it at all. His language really was quite highbrow."

A matter of weeks after being named in the *Daily Mail* all-star world team, Leigh was involved in the first of a number of controversial incidents that would not only dog the rest of his career but lead him into an ongoing feud with the game's ruling body in England. On Saturday 10 February 1906 Stoke made the long journey north to face Sunderland at Roker Park, the club's pre-Stadium of Light home. The game itself was uneventful, a 1-0 defeat leaving City adrift in mid-table following their promising start to the season. Afterwards players and officials from both sides came together in a building adjoining the ground to socialise over a post-match meal. At some point during the proceedings one of the diners, believed to be a guest of a Sunderland director, began shouting insults at the Stoke team. Despite being asked on several occasions to stop by members of the Sunderland party, the insults continued to come thick and fast. When the expression 'ten cads and a goalkeeper' came drifting across the room, the goalkeeper in question decided to do something about it. Rising from his chair, Leigh crossed over to where the man was sitting and punched him in the face.

At the subsequent FA inquiry into the incident held three weeks later, a long line of witnesses (including several from Sunderland) testified that Leigh had acted under severe provocation and should be spared any kind of punishment. Despite this the FA banned him from playing any football for a period of 14 days, beginning on 5 March. Leigh was furious at the decision but chose to accept it partly, it was rumoured, to spare his pacifist father any further embarrassment.

Other than making an official apology to Stoke City, Sunderland and the man in question during the inquiry, Leigh declined to talk publicly or write about the matter, refusing all invitations from journalists to give his side of the story. Instead it was left to the newspapers to defend his actions. 'As the incident occurred on the private premises of Sunderland, and not during the game, the sentence seems very severe', reported the *Athletic News*, capturing the national mood among the media and supporters. 'The fault did not lay all on one side, although we suppose the Football Association are acting as they deem wise in the interests of the game. It is possible to be too draconic'.

The FA's decision left Stoke City without their first-choice goalkeeper for two matches, both of which they lost to sink further down the First Division table. Wales, on the other hand, weren't so unfortunate. Leigh's two-week lay-off came into force 48 hours after their trip to Edinburgh to face Scotland in the Home Nations and expired the same day as England were due to play in Cardiff. Both games would prove to be pivotal moments in the development of Welsh football. The 2-0 win at Tynecastle Park, courtesy of second half goals from William Jones and John Love Jones, was the Principality's first ever victory north of the border, proof at last that Wales were ready to match the big boys on their own turf. Sixteen days later over 15,000 people flocked to Cardiff Arms Park for the England game. The visitors won by a single goal by Samuel Day but the occasion proved to be a moral victory for the Welsh who dominated for long spells despite missing their chief playmaker, Billy Meredith. The healthy attendance also silenced those sceptics who argued that football could never compete with rugby union for the sporting affections of the south Wales people.

On Monday 2 April Wales played their final Home Nations fixture of the year against Ireland at Wrexham. For Leigh and Fred McKee, his opposite number in the Irish goal, the afternoon proved to be something of a disaster, both men conceding four times in an eight-goal thriller which saw the visitors recover from 4-2 down with 15 minutes remaining. Much of the action was caught on camera by the Lancashire-based duo of Sagar Mitchell and James Kenyon who travelled the UK throughout the early 1900s making films about any subject that captured their imagination (the BBC would screen a three-part documentary about the pair in 2005 following the discovery of a stash of their work in a cellar in Blackburn).

Fortunately approximately two-and-a-half minutes of this footage survives today, officially recognised as the oldest anywhere in the world featuring an international football match. The film begins with players from both sides emerging from the dressing rooms at the Racecourse Ground and climbing over a low railing surrounding the pitch, several eyeballing the camera out of curiosity as they pass by. The referee and both linesmen, as with the majority of male spectators, are seen wearing peaked caps while the women in the 6,000-strong crowd promenade in long dresses, bonnets and wide-brimmed hats. The action on the pitch is shown at close quarters and includes four of the goals, in itself something of a feat considering the many changes of film roll that would have been necessary throughout the match. In one scene an unidentified Irish player collides with a goalpost while in the act of scoring, picking up what appears to be a groin strain in the process. As he collapses on the ground in agony a visibly annoyed Prince of Goalkeepers recovers the ball from the net and with one gigantic drop-kick sends it soaring into the distance towards the halfway line.

"In terms of its historical significance the film is absolutely priceless, being the earliest surviving footage of an international football match that we know of," says Vanessa Toulmin, co-curator of the Mitchell and Kenyon Collection. "What has survived is in such perfect condition that it looks as though it was filmed yesterday. It contains all the elements we associate with more advanced football coverage such as the teams running out onto the pitch, the action and the reaction of the crowd. We think shots of weeping Geordies and Scousers at football matches is a relatively new thing. Mitchell and Kenyon's footage tells us it's not. The only real disappointment is that Bill Meredith is missing from the action because he was suspended at the time and couldn't play. But Leigh Roose is there, captured for posterity. One thing you can really begin to appreciate by watching the film is how much danger goalkeepers were in at that time. Mitchell and Kenyon always liked to film corners being taken because they could almost guarantee where the action was about to take place. As a result they recorded many goalkeepers being physically battered by opposing players. It's hardly surprising that so many of them feared catching the ball, preferring instead to try and punch it clear."

It is worth noting that Mitchell and Kenyon edited their footage immediately so that players, supporters and officials could see themselves on camera in a tent adjoining the Racecourse Ground within an hour or two of the game finishing. The original film would have lasted around 15 minutes, with admission costing sixpence.

The silent images that survive today – now the property of the British Film Institute – are almost certainly the only moving pictures still in existence of Leigh Richmond Roose.

5

Glory Days

I T'S just gone midday on Monday 4 March 1907, exactly a year and day since the FA's inquiry into the Sunderland post-match fracas. Leigh Roose is leaning out of a second storey window at The Imperial Hotel in Wrexham. Down below the town's streets are beginning to fill with supporters arriving for this afternoon's clash between Wales and Scotland. Several take the opportunity to stop beneath Leigh's window and engage in a bit of banter. Will Wales finally win the Home Nations Championship? Is it true he is on the verge of leaving Stoke? Is London really as hedonistic as it's meant to be? Leigh deals with each in turn including a tongue-in-cheek marriage proposal courtesy of a woman alighting from a hansom cab (politely declined). Someone asks what today's score will be. "One to Wales, none to Scotland," comes the reply.

Fast forward nearly four hours. It's 0-0 with two minutes of the match remaining. Billy Meredith crosses the ball from the right flank to Gordon Jones. His shot is deflected by the St Mirren defender Thomas Jackson into the path of

Grenville Morris who tries his luck with a first time strike. Scotland's goalkeeper, Peter McBride, dives full length and manages to get his hands to the effort but it's too late. The ball is already at least a foot over the line. On the full time whistle Leigh removes both his boots and launches them into the ecstatic crowd.

Having already beaten Ireland 3-2 in Belfast two weeks previously, Wales are closing in on their first ever Home Nations Championship. All that stands between them and a place in the history books is the small matter of England in a fortnight's time at Craven Cottage, home of Fulham Football Club.

Back at The Imperial Hotel the party continues late into the evening. Leigh buys a round of drinks for everyone present (which no doubt will, like his room, be charged to the Football Association of Wales). A man attempts to reunite the goalkeeper with one of his boots but Leigh is having none of it, saying he can keep it as a souvenir. At some point after 11pm he bids his farewell and heads upstairs. On the first floor landing he is joined by two women who accompany Leigh into his room. Neither are seen to leave.

Thirteen days later and Leigh finds himself at Euston station awaiting the arrival of a special train from Wrexham conveying the Welsh team and some of their supporters to London. Tonight there will be no high jinks, just a meal at the side's hotel after which Leigh will return alone to his Mayfair apartment. The omens, it has to be said, don't look good for the following afternoon's game. Several key players including both first-choice full backs, Charlie Morris and Horace Blew, haven't made the trip due to a combination of frustrating circumstances. England, fielding a team consisting entirely of professionals, are at full strength. Perhaps now more than ever before Wales need Billy Meredith and Leigh Roose to be at their very best.

Despite it being a Monday around 1,000 people have travelled from Wales for the occasion with a sizeable London Welsh contingent also making their presence felt in the crowd of around 22,000. England make an uncharacteristically nervy start, their normally fluent play hampered by the strong easterly breeze sweeping up the adjacent River Thames. Wales sense they have a chance and with Meredith making a nuisance of himself on the right wing begin to create opportunities. One particularly dangerous cross grazes the England bar. Left winger Robert Evans manages to keep the ball in play. He looks up and spots Lot Jones standing unmarked in front of goal. The cross is an accurate one, Lot can hardly miss, and Wales have the lead. At the opposite end of the field Leigh, contrary to his flamboyant nature, shows no emotion whatsoever. He knows that with over an hour remaining there's still plenty of time for an English backlash.

Sure enough England dominate the second half and equalise through the Liverpool forward James Stewart following a mistake by Lloyd Davies. Yet Wales hold out for a draw and leave the field complaining about being denied a late penalty after Newcastle United forward John Rutherford had appeared to handle the ball inside his own penalty area. The result leaves Wales top of the table with five points from three games (under the old two points for a win system). However, England, boasting three points from two games, have one more fixture left to play. Victory over Scotland by two clear goals at St James' Park, Newcastle, on 6 April will be enough for them to pip Wales to the title.

Despite the uncertainty over who would finish first the press on the whole reacted to the 1-1 draw as though Wales had already won the Championship. 'The Welsh Assoc-iation football eleven have played with a fervour and unity of a brotherhood this season, and if they should be hailed as the champions of the Four Nations in the British Isles on April 6th nobody will begrudge them this rare distinction', reported the *Athletic News*. 'We do not suppose there will be bonfires on the tops of Snowdon down to the hill of Holyhead, but there will be a quiet sense of satisfaction'.

As it was Wales did end up winning their first ever Home Nations Championship. England put in a weak performance against the Scots with the game finishing 1-1. In a letter to his father, Leigh described the day as 'something of an anti-climax, being as we were scattered into all corners of the land, denied the opportunity to rejoice together as one'. Two weeks later that opportunity duly arose courtesy of the Football Association of Wales which threw a banquet in honour of the 21 players who had helped secure the title (each man receiving a commemorative medal made of Welsh gold in recognition of their efforts). Several players made brief speeches among them Leigh who dedicated his medal to the memory of his late brother Edward.

For a nation so low on resources and manpower, the Welsh 1907 Home Nations Championship win was a considerable achievement. In none of the three games had Wales managed to field the side originally selected, with failure to get players released by their English league clubs as much a problem as injury or sickness. Besides Leigh only four men – George Latham, Lloyd Davies, Lot Jones and Billy Meredith – were ever-present in the side. The Football Association of Wales hoped (forlornly, as it would emerge) that winning the title would encourage more English clubs to allow Welsh players leave of absence on international duty, together with boosting the sport's profile particularly in the south of the country. As a correspondent from *The Times* wrote on the eve of the 1907 banquet, 'If the Welsh Association can only develop Cardiff as seems possible and some of the more populous centres of the south, they might become as dreaded as their rugby brethren in the international tourney'. Sure enough that's exactly what began to happen. In 1906 the South Wales & Monmouth Football Association had 74 affiliated clubs on its books. By 1910 that number had soared to 262 competing across 12 divisions.

If there was a complaint to be made it remained the Welsh media's baffling refusal to embrace the round ball game, even a debut win in the Home Nations Championship failing to set pulses racing. The day after the England versus Scotland game the *South Wales Echo* ran a small match report covering events in Newcastle without the slightest mention of what the 1-1 draw had meant to Wales. This lack of recognition angered several of the players not to mention many followers of the sport. A watershed moment had been reached. Bowing to public pressure, the Welsh press would improve its football coverage immeasurably over the next couple of years.

As far as Leigh was concerned being a member of a Championship-winning side did little to raise his profile. He was, after all, already one of the most recognisable sporting faces in Britain. The only exception to the rule proved to be his birthplace of Holt. "I think that's when the penny dropped that we had a hero in our midst," recalled Arthur Tapp in 2000 shortly before his death. "Of course everyone knew him as this tall, quite imposing but friendly chap and was proud of him being the Welsh international goalkeeper, but perhaps we didn't realise how good he really was or how highly regarded he was everywhere else. Winning the

Championship changed that. His trips back home became events, particularly among us local boys. We couldn't get enough of him. Everyone wanted to meet and talk to him."

There couldn't have been a greater contrast between club and country for Leigh during the spring of 1907. While Wales basked in the glory of their first title, Stoke were marooned at the bottom of the First Division and fast running out of games in which to save themselves. The debts had continued to spiral out of control to the point where no one seemed to know exactly how much was owed to who, for what, and from when. City's relegation was confirmed on a rainy Saturday in mid-April following a 2-0 home defeat to Middlesbrough in front of just 4,000 despondent people.

The recriminations began more or less immediately. And it came as no surprise to discover Leigh directing traffic in the middle of it all. Having wrongly assumed that the club's financial problems were a distant memory, the news that Stoke were going back on their promise of an unlimited expense account had almost caused him to walk out on the club for a second time in February. A compromise was struck with Leigh reducing his monetary demands on condition that whatever weekly claim he made was settled prior to games. No pay, no play. This continued until the Monday after the Middlesbrough game when, in an interview with the *Athletic News*, an unnamed club source attributed Stoke's relegation to certain senior players 'not doing their duty', especially in light of the 'considerable recompense provided for their services'. Recognising a slur when he read one, Leigh told friends he would never play for the club again.

Stung by further criticism of gross financial misman-agement from supporters and the press, the club then released further details of illegal expenses claims demanded by some of their amateur players, ones that Stoke – desperate to appear whiter than white – insisted they had turned down. They included a claim from a London-based player who had asked for money to pay someone to look after his dog while away on duty with the club, even though he didn't have a dog. Stoke only had one London-based player and the Football Association knew it. From that point the sport's governing body in England would be on Leigh's case like a hawk, something he would never forgive Stoke for.

Throughout the summer an uneasy stand-off continued between club and player. Away from the football field Leigh had his degree finals at King's to concentrate on. He passed but with little fanfare (college records show him to have won none of the sought after academic prizes competed for by enthusiastic undergraduates). Keen to remain in medicine but reluctant to spend the next two years studying to become a fully-fledged doctor, Leigh chose instead to work as a research assistant in the bacteriology departments at various London hospitals including King's and Imperial. Once the football career was over and done with, then he would complete those two missing years. At least that's what he told family and friends. Whether he really meant it, we will never know.

Given everything that had gone before, one of the biggest shocks on the opening day of the 1907/08 season in September was Leigh's appearance for Stoke in their Second Division fixture against Clapton Orient, the slight thaw in relations being down to the resignation of two of the club's directors. Although some papers reported that he had promised to stay at City for the rest of the season (something which according to the *Athletic News* would 'give unqualified satisfaction in north Staffordshire where he is one of the most popular players who has ever worn the Stoke colours'), in reality there was more chance of pigs flying. With City's better players already having jumped ship for clubs in the First Division, Leigh – by now at the peak of his career – was never going to waste a whole year playing in English football's second tier.

The following month, Leigh quit Stoke for good.

As someone who for six years had spent a large portion of his weekends on trains simply getting to and from football matches (the round trips to Stoke and Liverpool from London are approximately 340 and 440 miles respectively) you would have forgiven Leigh for wanting his next port of call to be slightly closer to home. As it was, it could hardly have been further away.

In the years following their admission to the Football League in 1890, Sunderland had come to be regarded as one of the most powerful football forces in the land. The club had finished top of the First Division in 1892, 1893 and 1895 with a side that became known as the 'Team of all the Talents', capturing the title once again in 1902. At home they were particularly strong, suffering just a single defeat during one remarkable six-year stretch and regularly walloping visiting sides by six, seven or even eight goals.

For 14 seasons spanning the years 1890 to 1904 successive Sunderland sides had been built around one man, a prematurely balding Scotsman by the name of Teddy Doig, the original 'Prince of Goalkeepers' before Leigh's arrival on the scene. Although nowhere near as adventurous in his play or statuesque in build as Leigh there's no doubt

Doig was a brilliant keeper, described by one journalist as being 'as cool as a cucumber between the posts'. Legend has it that at the height of his fame he even received a letter from a fan delivered to his home with the single word 'Doig' written on it surrounded by a set of goalposts.

After 674 league, cup and friendly appearances it's hardly surprising that Doig's decision to leave Sunderland for Second Division Liverpool left a huge void. Many felt it was the catalyst for the club's decline post-1904 during which their league position slipped year by year and they rarely survived beyond the first round of the FA Cup. With relegation by now looking a distinct possibility, manager Bob Kyle set out to reverse Sunderland's fortunes by rebuilding the team, starting from the back. And Leigh, now without a club, was his number one target as goalkeeper.

Despite the huge distance from London to the north-east of England, not to mention the 'ten cads and a goalkeeper' post-match skirmish the previous year, Leigh had little hesitation in accepting Kyle's offer. Even allowing for their poor recent form, Sunderland were a club with pedigree. Having played at their Roker Park ground on several occasions, he had also witnessed first-hand the passion of the local people for their team. Crowds of between 15,000 and 20,000 (double that on the days when rivals Newcastle United came to town) were the norm, just the kind of stage a born entertainer dreams of. The large attendances also meant the club had no qualms about agreeing to or meeting Leigh's considerable expenses claims.

With England international forwards George Holley and Arthur Bridgett in their side, Sunderland were never going to struggle scoring goals (they would finish the 1907/08 season as the First Division's second highest goalscorers behind champions Manchester United). Keeping them out, however, was something altogether different. Leigh's arrival in January 1908 certainly helped plug some of the gaps, but with the rest of the defence either short on confidence or nearing the end of their careers Sunderland were still conceding far too many for comfort. Over the ensuing year Kyle's recruitment of centre back and Scotland captain Charlie Thomson, full back Albert Milton and half back Harry Low would help take the weight off the Sunderland keeper's shoulders. But to say Leigh was a busy man during those first few months is a gross understatement. Not that he complained. That was exactly the way he liked it.

As ever with Leigh, controversy was never far away. That March, just days after he was knocked unconscious by Tottenham forward Vivian Woodward during the early stages of Wales' Home Nations match with England at Wrexham, the Football Association launched an inquiry into the goalkeeper's expenses claims. The FA rules regarding payments to amateur players were simple – they shouldn't happen. Stoke's decision the previous summer to publicise details of alleged illegal expenses claims demanded by some of their amateur players had given the FA enough ammunition to act on something they had long suspected; that Leigh was a professional in everything but name.

Far from being concerned, Leigh treated the matter with complete contempt. Asked to compile a list of each individual claim submitted so far during the 1907/08 season, he included the following:

> Pistol to ward off opposition…4d
> Coat and gloves to keep warm when not occupied…3d
> Using the toilet (twice)…2d

Somehow Sunderland managed to wangle their way out of any trouble by producing receipts showing that the club simply paid his travel expenses and nothing else. It was a farce, yet the FA were powerless to do anything about it.

Even the media, seemingly blind to the true nature of some of Leigh's outrageous demands, appeared to side with the goalkeeper. One correspondent in the *Athletic News* wrote, 'It is an open secret that the Football Association have enquired into his relationship with Sunderland. To some people, the fact that an amateur consents to play in a professional team without reward is incomprehensible. We rejoice in amateurs like Roose, Arthur Berry, G H Barlow, W S Corbett, W J Woodward and many in the Southern League that do play professional football. We should like to see more of them in the ranks, as we are convinced that they do the game good. He (Leigh) is in the game for sport, and for the sheer love of football'.

Sunderland's risky decision not just to help bankroll Leigh's lavish bachelor lifestyle but also to cover for him in the face of an FA inquiry would, however, pay dividends on the football field. Five victories from their final seven league games, including a fine 3-1 win over Newcastle at St James' Park in front of 50,000 spectators, saw the club escape relegation by two points. As a thank you gesture to the one player he believed had done more than any other to help the club beat the drop, Sunderland chairman John Wilson sought approval for a testimonial game to be played at Roker Park in Leigh's honour, the gate money from which would go to the goalkeeper. At this point the FA saw an opportunity to exact some revenge over the expenses matter and turned down Wilson's request. Only professionals, it said, could benefit from testimonial games.

Instead a gala dinner attended by players, directors and local dignitaries was held two weeks after the final game of the season, during which Leigh was presented with a highly decorative leather-bound document (referred to by the club as an 'address') containing four pages, one of which was inscribed with the following words:

On behalf of the inhabitants of Sunderland &
District we, the members of
the Testimonial Committee, ask your acceptance
of this address as an expression
of our appreciation of the very valuable services
you rendered to the Sunderland Association
Football Club during the 1907/08 season.
We feel that the satisfactory position eventually
obtained by the club in the league
table at the end of the season was largely due to
the splendid and masterly exposition
of goal defence shown by you at the most critical
period in the club's history. Nor can
we forget the services you so generously gave to
the club, or overlook the confidence
which you inspired among the other members of
the team.
We trust that your connection with the club will,
as hitherto, be harmonious and
pleasant, and in the name of a very large and
representative body of subscribers,
we offer our most hearty good wishes for your
future welfare.

The remaining three pages carried a picture of the Borough of Sunderland coat of arms (carrying the motto *Nil Desperandum Auspice Deo*, or 'With God on our side, we cannot fail'), a head and shoulders portrait of Leigh, and the signatures of each member of the club's Testimonial Committee. The document, still in excellent condition, is now in the possession of Leigh's great-nephew, Nick

Jenkins, himself a former Lieutenant Colonel in The Royal Green Jackets and housemaster at Shrewsbury School.

Having created the mother of all impressions inside the space of just five months, Leigh was never going to consider trading Sunderland in for another club that summer. Respected by his teammates, adored by the town's public and playing some of the best football of his life, it's hardly surprising that family and close friends remember him being at his happiest around this time. Not even the long round trip to and from the north-east for every home game could dampen Leigh's spirits. Allowing for a change at Newcastle, there were two early trains from London's King's Cross station on a Saturday that could get him to Sunderland with time to spare before kick-off. Occasionally things went slightly awry.

There was the morning when he missed both departures and in a panic took it upon himself to hire his own steam locomotive plus one carriage to convey him the entire way (unfortunately there is no record of Sunderland's reaction to this on being presented with the bill!). His nephew, Dick Jenkins, distinctly remembered another occasion towards the end of his stay with Sunderland when Leigh arrived at King's Cross just as the second train was pulling out of the station. Unperturbed, he hurdled a barrier, sprinted along the platform until level with the last coach, opened a door and climbed inside.

With manager Bob Kyle continuing to bring in new recruits, much was expected of Sunderland ahead of the 1908/09 season. Although they began poorly with a 4-2 defeat at Bury and went on to suffer further reverses to Chelsea, Blackburn and Everton during October and November, Kyle's side nevertheless entered December in sixth place, the pick of their victories being the 6-1 mauling of defending champions Manchester United plus an equally impressive 4-0 win at Woolwich Arsenal.

On 5 December Sunderland made the short trip to Newcastle for the 21st league clash between the local rivals. It's a date that well over a century later remains one of the proudest in the history of the Wearside club, and one of the more forgettable on the banks of the River Tyne. Why? Because it marks Sunderland's biggest away win of all time, and Newcastle's heaviest defeat ever at home.

Two weeks previously Newcastle had lost 2-0 at St James' Park to Aston Villa and consequently decided to drop five senior players for the visit of Sunderland including England forward John Rutherford and Scottish winger Peter McWilliam. Even so, the game was expected to be close. The 56,000 spectators packed inside the ground saw Billy Hogg give the visitors an early lead, with Newcastle drawing level on the stroke of half-time thanks to a controversial penalty from Albert Shepherd, Sunderland insisting the ball had hit captain Charlie Thomson's hand outside the box.

Perhaps this grievance helped inspire Sunderland for the second period because what followed was – and remains – little short of astonishing. As the heavens opened on an already heavy pitch, so George Holley made it 2-1 to Sunderland. Hogg added another for 3-1, followed straight from the restart by a fourth from Holley. Hogg and Holley then completed their hat-tricks, inspiring Arthur Bridgett to get in on the act with a further two goals. Jackie Mordue completed the scoring to make the final score Newcastle United 1 Sunderland 9, eight of which had come within the space of 28 incredible minutes.

In his book *Into the Light*, Roger Hutchinson describes how a Sunderland reserve team game was taking place at

Roker Park on the same afternoon. As updates from St James' Park were displayed on a scoreboard, the supporters present greeted each goal with a loud cheer. That is until the fifth went in at which point the crowd fell silent, convinced they were the victims of some elaborate hoax. For the record, Newcastle finished the season as league champions having shipped 41 goals in 38 games. Almost a quarter of those were conceded on 5 December 1908 alone.

'When some beardless boys have become grandfathers, they will gather the younger generation round them and tell a tale of Tyneside, about 11 stalwart Sunderland footballers who travelled to St James' Park and thrashed the famous Novocastrians as if they had been a poor lot of unfortunates from some home for the blind', wrote journalist James Catton of the occasion. 'The greatest match of this season provided the sensation of the year and we shall have to turn back the days to when the game was in its infancy for a parallel performance. Never have I watched forwards who have seized their opportunities with more eagerness and unerring power'.

The game finished with Leigh in possession of the match ball. Afterwards he refused to part with it, aware of its potential value and historical significance. The following morning he returned to London where he presented it to his nephew, then just three and a half years old. "I don't actually remember him giving it to me, but the ball was always around at home," recalled Dick Jenkins, the nephew in question. "Being a child, and not living near the north-east, I never really recognised its significance. I kept it until World War Two. I went abroad, served in Burma, got shot twice, came home, moved house, and at some point realised it wasn't around anymore. It must have got lost when we changed addresses."

Newcastle United would prove to be a recurring theme of the 1908/09 season for Sunderland. In March the two sides drew each other in the quarter-finals of the FA Cup at St James' Park. The match was an absolute classic, later described by Arthur Appleton (the BBC's former 'Voice of football' in the north-east and a keen historian of the local game) as the greatest played at the ground up until that time. Although James Catton, once again assigned by the *Athletic News* to cover the Tyne/Wear derby, wrote that 'Sunderland's backs never inspired confidence', adding 'it must be a trial for Roose to keep goal behind men whose movements give cause for such wonderment', the general consensus was that the sheer pace of what culminated in a 2-2 draw meant both sets of players were out on their feet come the final whistle.

The replay four days later at Roker Park saw Newcastle progress to the semi-finals with a 3-0 win, the result swinging on a penalty save by United's goalkeeper Jimmy Lawrence from George Holley. But at least Sunderland had the consolation the following month of completing a league double over their neighbours thanks to a 3-1 home win. Victories in their final two games including an impressive 4-2 away success against FA Cup finalists Bristol City meant they finished the season in third place, hardly earth shattering considering Sunderland's outstanding feats the previous decade but still a vast improvement on 12 months previously.

On the international scene Wales also had cause to celebrate. After the high of 1907 they proceeded to lose all three of their Home Nations fixtures the following year, having to make do without Leigh for 55 minutes of the England match and all of the Ireland game three weeks later due to injury. However, the spring of 1909 saw Wales bounce back to win two out of three internationals, their only defeat (2-0 against England at Nottingham) sandwiched between 3-2 victories over Scotland at Wrexham and Ireland in Belfast. The latter proved to be especially memorable, played as it was against the backdrop of one of Leigh's choicest practical jokes.

"In those days, Wales was never really sure of a first team and there used to be a sigh of relief when the party trickled up in twos or threes," Billy Meredith later recalled. "Reserves were usually standing by, but a reserve goalkeeper was not thought of when Dick Roose (Meredith always called Leigh 'Dick') was holding down the position. You can imagine the consternation then when he turned up at Liverpool for the boat to Belfast with his hand heavily bandaged. He told everyone not to worry, that he'd only broken a couple of bones but would be able to play. Those of us who knew him well were naturally suspicious and when we settled in our hotel in Belfast, Charlie Morris and I peeped through the keyhole of his room and saw him unwind the bandage and exercise his fingers. Next morning he appeared with his bandage back on and the telegraph wires hummed with the news that the Welsh goalkeeper was going to play with two broken fingers. The photographers crowded around the Welsh goal at the start of the match but once the play was in progress Dick calmly unwound the bandage and went on to play his usual blinder!"

6

The Good, the Bad and the Injury

BY 1909 football in Britain at the highest level was changing fast. The amateur era was almost over, with Leigh Roose the most high profile of a diminishing band of men still playing for the love of the game plus whatever expenses they chose to seek. Football grounds, until now little more than pitches surrounded by fences and man-made banks for spectators to stand on, were being redeveloped into large arenas capable of holding many thousands of people featuring mod cons such as seating and covered terracing. What's more, fans were beginning to travel the length and breadth of the country following their clubs, taking advantage of relatively affordable travel on an extensive and increasingly efficient railway network.

Not all the changes were for the better. The coming together of large numbers of people supporting opposing teams had led to a spate of crowd control problems and the

Leigh Roose.

The Manse, Holt – birthplace of Leigh Roose.

The former Holt Academy where, according to H G Wells, "lessons took place with the uncertainty of April showers."

Vicarage Fields, Aberystwyth, where Leigh honed many of his goalkeeping skills and female students from the University of Wales flocked to watch him play.

The final resting place of Leigh's brother Edward Roose, St Chad's Church, Holt.

Wales line up ahead of their 1901 fixture against England with Leigh standing in the middle row, third from left. His close friend Billy Meredith is holding the ball in the front row.

Leigh in action, 1905.

The original net-minder. Leigh at home in familiar surroundings.

Waiting for the ball.

A picture of Leigh from a cigarette card.

A cartoon from 1909 showing Leigh in his Sunderland kit, drawn by Lee Bennett for the Liverpool Weekly Courier.

Wales line up ahead of their 1907 clash against Scotland, the year Leigh and his team-mates won the Home International Championships for the first time in the Principality's history. Leigh is in the front row with the ball between his knees.

Dick Jenkins with the address presented to Leigh in 'appreciation of the very valuable services you rendered to the Sunderland Association Football Club during the season 1907/08'.

The Thiepval Memorial.

The fields to the north of Gueudecourt showing the area where on 7 October 1916 332 officers and soldiers of the 9th Royal Fusiliers were killed or injured. The scrub on the left marks the line of Bayonet Trench, the first objective that day for Allied troops who attacked from the area shown on the right-hand side of both pictures.

The grave of an unknown Royal Fusilier in the cemetery at Flers.

Welsh football historian Gil Jones lays a cross at the foot of the Thiepval Memorial in memory of Leigh.

Schoolboys from St Joseph's School in Wrexham line up at the Racecourse Ground in 2006 before recreating the Wales versus Ireland game from 100 years previously (pictures courtesy of Wales Screen).

John Toshack alongside the plaque displaying Leigh's face celebrating Mitchell and Kenyon's historic film from 1906 (picture courtesy of Wales Screen).

Leigh's great-nephew and great-niece, Nick Jenkins and Gaynor Tinsdale, at Holt War Memorial, 2015.

Leigh's name on Holt War Memorial, 2015.

At long last. Leigh's name spelled correctly on the Thiepval Memorial, 2015.

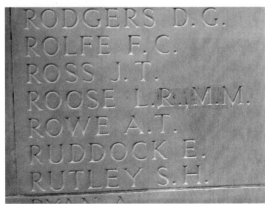

first real examples of football hooliganism. One of the most notable incidents occurred when Newcastle United came to Roker Park on 18 September 1909. The game kicked off in muggy conditions and with more people on the terraces than there was adequate room for. On four separate occasions during the opening 20 minutes the referee was forced to bring play to a halt because spectators had spilled onto the pitch. Leigh himself almost collided with a fan while in the process of catching a high cross. When the local mounted police attempted to push the crowd back one of the horses was stabbed with a knife, causing the animal to stampede around the playing field leading to yet another delay. Despite the offer of a substantial reward, the culprit was never caught.

One aspect of the game that had remained constant over the years was Leigh's attack-minded style of goalkeeping, running out as far as the halfway line while in possession of the ball before releasing it with one giant kick or throw. Although other keepers had by now become more adventurous in their play, using the whole of the penalty area rather than staying rooted to their line waiting for a shot, Leigh was still in a world of his own when it came to using 50 per cent of the pitch. This baffled him. "The law states that any custodian is free to run over half of the field of play before ridding themselves of the ball," he said in 1909. "This not only helps to puzzle the attacking forwards but to build the foundation for swift, incisive counter-attacking play. Why then do so few make use of it?"

Leigh's Sunderland teammate George Holley thought he knew the answer. 'He was the only one who did it because he was the only one who could kick or throw a ball that accurately over long distances, giving himself time to return to his goal without fear of conceding', Holley wrote a few years before his death in 1942. 'He knew he was good, but I don't think he ever realised exactly how good he really was'.

The press, however, failed to share Holley's positive take on Leigh's forays upfield, regarding it as the goalkeeper's one true weakness. 'The great man of the side was Roose', reported the *Athletic News* following Sunderland's 4-1 win over Liverpool in September 1909, before adding, 'His one failing is his habit of running out with the ball, a failing which I suppose will ever be with him, but he is a brilliant goalkeeper without doubt'. Mistakes, though few and far between, helped fuel the media's stance. The following month at Bramall Lane a long punt by Sheffield United's veteran goalkeeper Ernest Needham caught Leigh completely out of position, the ball sailing over his head into the Sunderland net. Yet the Welshman, in his carefree way, simply laughed the incident off. "I ought to give up when I let an old man of 40 score with a shot like that," he told Needham afterwards before buying him a congratulatory drink.

Nor did the odd mistake stop him from continuing to show off to the crowds. In one match at Aston Villa, Leigh pushed a powerful long range shot over the crossbar, catching hold of the wooden beam in the same movement and pulling himself up onto it with the agility of a gymnast. Once there he sat milking the applause from around the ground before jumping back down again to face the resulting corner kick. Against Woolwich Arsenal at Roker Park – with Sunderland leading 5-2 – he blocked a shot with his chest, brought the falling ball to rest balancing on his right foot, and embarked on a spot of keepy-uppy.

Although sailing dangerously close to unsportsmanlike behaviour, opposing players tended to regard Leigh's antics with as much amusement as supporters who continued to be subjected to the goalkeeper's jocular banter during matches.

"Who wants to buy me dinner afterwards?" he bellowed to spectators stood behind his goal while waiting for the referee to start the second half of a game at Notts County. "But you wouldn't know if he was serious," said teammate Charlie Thomson who had been stood nearby at the time and overheard the remark. "He was an extremely friendly chap who enjoyed the company of all sorts of people, so he may well have been."

Not content with merely appearing on the sports pages, Leigh's name was also starting to crop up in newspaper gossip columns. Towards the end of 1909 he began being seen around London with the singer Marie Lloyd, queen of the country's music halls known simply to her adoring public as 'Our Marie'. At the time Lloyd was one of the most famous women in Britain, as much for the suggestive songs she performed (punctuated by saucy winks and knowing looks) as the sound of her voice. With her second marriage to the singer Alec Hurley in trouble, it wasn't long before people began putting two and two together regarding her and Leigh.

Even by today's celebrity obsessed standards, they made a dream showbiz couple – the darling of the music hall stage, her neat features draped in the finest clothes, on the arm of the broad-shouldered, handsome, 6ft-plus football player. Little effort was made to hide their liaisons despite Lloyd still being married. When she performed, Leigh would take time out to go and watch her. When Sunderland came to London, so Lloyd would repay the compliment. One evening Leigh's sister Helena returned home from church to find the pair sat drinking tea together in her drawing room. "I think she was absolutely flabbergasted," her son Dick would recall a little over 90 years later. "It's not every day you arrive home to discover the country's most celebrated singer there waiting to meet you."

Though clearly more than just friends, there is however little real evidence that this was anything other than a fling on both sides. Now 32, Leigh was still showing zero interest in shedding his bachelor ways while Lloyd's tangled love life was already the stuff of Edwardian legend. By the summer of 1910 the relationship was over, Lloyd having met and supposedly fallen in love with a young jockey called Bernard Dillon who had ridden Lemburg to victory in that year's Derby. Following Hurley's death in 1914 Dillon became her third husband, although the couple would separate six years later largely as a result of their respective drink problems (Dillon had also been charged in 1920 with assaulting his father-in-law). Broken-hearted and by now a full-blown alcoholic, Lloyd continued performing despite her rapidly deteriorating health, her voice becoming weaker and performances shorter. On 4 October 1922 she collapsed on stage in the north London suburb of Edmonton. Three days later, she was dead.

No matter how casual their relationship had been, Leigh would owe Lloyd one huge debt. Being seen out and about with 'Our Marie' meant his profile hit new heights. People who had never been to a game of football or read the sports pages now knew all about Leigh Richmond Roose, the pin-up boy of Edwardian sport. The *Daily Mail* dubbed him 'London's most eligible bachelor', second only to the Surrey and England cricketer Jack Hobbs in a top 10 list of the 'most recognisable sportsmen in the United Kingdom'. It all helped add a few extra numbers to the attendance wherever Leigh played. And the higher the gate, the more money he could command in expenses.

In truth the *Daily Mail*'s most eligible bachelor tag could just as easily have applied to several towns and cities other than London. Leigh's home may have been in the English capital but football commitments meant he was rarely there for longer than four or five days at a time. In the wake of his affair with Marie Lloyd, Sunderland Football Club was inundated with fan mail from women across the United Kingdom wanting to marry, have sex with, mother or go on a date with the Prince of Goalkeepers. The bulk of the correspondence came from upper working class and lower middle class women in their twenties and thirties, some of whom took their interest a step further by seeking Leigh out at his favourite hotels wherever Sunderland or Wales happened to be playing. We will never know how many were invited to join him for drinks, dinner or to share his bed, safe to say it was many. Sunderland's players used to joke that Leigh had a favourite girl or three in every port the team set sail for, a line that stemmed from his fondness for travelling to away games 24 hours early in order to spend the night in a hotel (at the club's expense) with an admirer, frequently delaying his return to London until the day after the match for the same reason.

Having finished the 1908/09 campaign in third position, Sunderland's patchy form the following season came as a big disappointment to their supporters who had expected the club to mount a challenge for the title. Instead they got mid-table mediocrity with flashes of brilliance one week followed by frustration personified the next. However, Leigh was once again in fine form, frequently keeping them in games they had no right to deserve anything from.

Two performances in particular during the course of the season came to be regarded as among his finest ever. The first helped deliver a valuable point in a 0-0 draw against top of the table Blackburn Rovers on 6 November. In the following Monday's *Athletic News*, James Catton wrote 'Leigh Richmond Roose was a superman among men, and he stood alone between Blackburn and the honour they coveted. What would have happened to Sunderland in this encounter without such a guardian, I hesitate to think. Whether the shots were straight or oblique, high or low, hurtling like cannonballs or sneaking surprises, Roose was at the ready. Valiant though volatile, dextrous though daring, he stands forth as one of the most glorious goalkeepers of modern times'.

It was much the same story two months later away to Woolwich Arsenal, only this time Leigh's heroics helped inspire Sunderland to somehow win the match 2-1. One correspondent present wrote 'From the Woolwich point of view, Leigh Richmond Roose was the destroying engine of Saturday's peace. William Buckenham led the Arsenal attack in a way that he has never approached before. On several occasions he burst clean through the Sunderland defence. He was yards faster than any of the northern backs, and (Charlie) Thomson could not hold them. But there was one man who could, and that was Roose. At least half a dozen times during the game, Roose had to repel shots taken at about six feet range by either Buckenham or a colleague, and each and every one he stopped. I have no doubt that Roose will be a nightmare to several of the Woolwich forwards for some time'.

All of which made the error-strewn, crazy months that were March and April 1910 all the more remarkable. Three games, none involving Sunderland, each encapsulating the dark side of both Leigh's goalkeeping and character. The first took place on 5 March at Kilmarnock during Wales' Home Nations fixture against Scotland. With four minutes remaining and the scoreline goalless, Falkirk's Andrew Devine opted to try his luck with a shot from 40 yards out. Why? Because he had spotted Leigh stood with his back towards play talking to a spectator. Charlie Morris of Derby County shouted to warn his goalkeeper but it was too late. The ball was already on its way into the net. They may have been close friends but a furious Billy Meredith let Leigh feel the full force of his anger immediately after the goal had been scored and again in the Welsh dressing room afterwards, although the rest of the squad – perhaps mindful of the number of times Roose had saved them – held back. It proved to be the only goal of the game.

Despite this lapse Leigh was then asked by Glasgow Celtic Football Club if he would be prepared to play as a stopgap goalkeeper in their Scottish Cup semi-final against Clyde the following weekend. As Sunderland were without a game, he agreed. Leigh did everything expected of him that day – talk to the crowds outside the ground before kick-off, pace restlessly backwards and forwards across his penalty area muttering under his breath – except have a good game. In fact he had a howler conceding three goals as Celtic crashed out of the cup, two of which were his fault. On leaving the pitch after the final whistle it was alleged Leigh also traded insults with a Celtic supporter unhappy at his performance. Instead of staying the night in a Glasgow hotel as planned, he slipped away as quietly as possible immediately afterwards and caught an overnight train back to London.

But both of these hiccups pale into insignificance compared to the events of Tuesday 23 April, without doubt the most controversial day in Leigh's entire playing career. Once again he had been asked to guest for another side in an important game. The side in question was Port Vale's reserve team who were set to face Stoke City's reserves at the Victoria Ground to decide the destiny of the North Staffordshire & District League title. It was a midweek match which involved taking a day off work, but that didn't bother Leigh. This was, after all, the ideal opportunity to get one over on Stoke, the club he still harboured a grudge against for the way they had treated him following their relegation to the Second Division three years previously.

Leigh was one of five ringers in the Port Vale team, another being Herbert Chapman who would go on to become a hugely successful manager building league championship winning sides at both Huddersfield Town and Arsenal. The concept of 'ringers' – bringing in outside players to increase a team's chances of winning – went completely against the spirit of the game and was guaranteed to antagonise the majority of the 7,000-plus crowd who turned up to watch the match that afternoon. However, it was Leigh's presence that would act as the catalyst for what followed, the fuse being well and truly lit when he took to the field wearing a Stoke shirt. City's players complained and the referee ordered him to change into a white top. Leigh, as though spoiling for some kind of confrontation, refused.

Hardly surprisingly given the strength of their side, Port Vale dominated the game and cruised into a 2-0 half-time lead. After the restart Stoke fought back but were unable to find a way past Leigh. At some point around the hour mark City's fans decided they had been humiliated enough and invaded the pitch, ignoring pleas from the police and their own players to remain behind the barriers. The seething mass made a beeline for their former idol, forcing the goalkeeper to escape in the direction of the nearby River Trent. According to *The Argus*, 'The Revd A E Hurst (Stoke's chairman) made a public appeal to the crowd to desist and, with the aid of the police and some of the Port Vale supporters, Roose was able to prise himself away from a watery grave and into the sanctuary of the dressing room.

As the crowd continued to swirl around the pitch like an angry mob, the Reverend made another appeal for the pitch to be cleared. As further progress proved impossible in the main match, two junior teams came out and started an exhibition game. The pitch cleared'.

At the subsequent inquiry held a week later Port Vale's secretary demanded that the game be awarded to his club, while Stoke accused Vale of being 'unsportsmanlike and contemptible' for scouring the country in search of suitable ringers. Stoke also countered accusations of failing to control the crowd properly by pointing out that they had increased the police presence from the usual three officers to eight. Unfortunately all eight were new to the job with just weeks of experience between them but that, as Stoke were at pains to point out, hadn't been the club's fault.

Leigh then delivered his *pièce de résistance*. Speaking through the Reverend Hurst who had agreed to act as his representative, Leigh claimed he had been under the impression that the game was just a friendly, not a title decider. The inquiry had no alternative but to accept his word leaving the FA unable to discipline him for inciting the crowd. Instead the title was declared void, Vale fined 10 shillings and Stoke's ground closed for the opening two weeks of the 1910/11 season. Fortunately for Leigh the national press seemed relatively uninterested in parochial midweek reserve team games no matter how violent they became, and both the initial incident and the inquiry went virtually unreported outside Staffordshire. However, the whole unsavoury business cost Leigh the respect of the Stoke supporters who had once adored him, a big price to pay for a football player in the name of revenge.

There is no record of how Sunderland felt about their first-choice goalkeeper, one they paid considerable expenses to employ, appearing for other clubs. As Leigh remained an amateur, free to play for whoever he chose, they would have been powerless to do anything about it anyway except perhaps for dropping him from the first team, something that would have been unpopular with supporters. Thankfully for the Wearsiders he emerged from his excursions with Wales, Celtic and Port Vale's reserves free from injury, helping Sunderland to an eighth place finish in the table. May 1910 also saw the FA, clearly stung by Leigh's excuses during the Stoke versus Port Vale inquiry, launch a second investigation into his dubious expenses claims. This time he simply didn't bother responding to their letters, with Sunderland once again stating they only paid his travel expenses plus any overnight accommodation bills should the goalkeeper need a bed either before or after a game. It was almost as though he was untouchable.

Despite suffering another relatively disappointing season compared to their glory days of the 1890s, Sunderland's popularity as a club was continuing to grow. Attendances were rising steadily and manager Bob Kyle had little difficulty in attracting some of Britain's best players, the exciting Everton forward Tim Coleman being the most notable arrival during the summer of 1910. Their finances were also in a healthy state with hundreds of pounds being spent renovating the stands and pitch, while the directors themselves had clubbed together to raise the £10,000 necessary to buy the ground, preventing it from falling into the hands of builders. When Leigh announced that he would continue to make the long round trip from London for another season, it only added to the growing feeling around Roker Park that the 1910/11 campaign could be Sunderland's year.

Coleman got off to a flying start at home to Newcastle United on the opening day, marking his debut with one of the goals in a 2-1 win. Consecutive victories followed against Sheffield Wednesday, Aston Villa and Oldham putting the Wearsiders top of the league with their best start to a campaign yet. Come 21 November, the day of the return game against Newcastle at St James' Park, Sunderland were still unbeaten and beginning to look like title certainties. Only once had Kyle's side looked fallible and even then they had managed to get out of jail, scraping a 3-3 draw at Manchester City despite half the team (including Leigh, who was held responsible for two of City's goals) having an off day. During the home wins against Everton and Bristol City the goalkeeper had been reduced to the role of a virtual spectator. It almost seemed to be going too smoothly.

The turning point not just of Sunderland's season but also of Leigh's entire football career came 15 minutes from the end of the match at Newcastle. With the score delicately balanced at 1-1, the England international Albert Shepherd took a shot which Leigh managed to cling onto at the second attempt. In doing so he was challenged by the United forward John Rutherford who attempted to kick the ball out of his hands. Players from both sides piled in, just in case the keeper should let it slip from his grasp. Leigh, however, lay motionless on the ground, his right arm wrapped tightly around the ball, his left broken just above the wrist. Referee Tom Campbell was one of the first to realise the severity of the injury, bringing play to a halt by running into the melee and standing directly over the stricken goalkeeper. A medic was sent for and players from both sides gathered round to see what had happened.

After a short delay Leigh was helped to his feet to warm applause from the 60,000 capacity crowd before being led from the pitch. The centre forward Arthur Bridgett took over between the posts and Sunderland managed to hold out until the final whistle for a point. Yet once inside the dressing room any sense of satisfaction at the result quickly disappeared as the implications of Leigh's injury began to sink in. He would be out for weeks, possibly even months. George Holley told one waiting reporter that it was a "worse disaster than a defeat." The incident had been a complete accident. Leigh told Rutherford as much when the forward came to see him immediately afterwards. But that would be of little consolation to Sunderland's players over the coming games as they faced up to life without the Prince.

A measure of Leigh's stature within the game was demonstrated by the vast amount of newspaper column inches devoted to what had happened at Newcastle. From some over the top tributes you could easily have been mistaken for thinking he had died, not merely broken an arm. James Catton was one journalist who managed to keep things in perspective. 'It has been said that all first class goalkeepers are among the mentally afflicted, but Roose suffers from a form of madness that gives joy to thousands of spectators, and no one but himself is a penny the worse', he wrote in the following Monday's *Athletic News*. 'We hope that this mishap will not terminate his career. Sunderland have Robert Allan, a Glasgow man of goodly proportions, to fall back upon and we hope that he will be as jealous of his reputation beneath the crossbar as Roose has been'.

Rather than travel back to London to have the arm treated by a familiar face in the medical profession, Leigh went straight to hospital in Newcastle for attention before returning south. Then it was just a matter of being patient until the arm mended. No football, and for the time being no bacteriology either. With so much spare time on his hands, Leigh's thoughts inevitably turned towards whether or not he would ever play top class football again. In an interview with James Catton, he said 'All good goalkeepers carry about them an air of invincibility, so it comes as the strangest sensation to realise that we are mortal after all. It is a helpless predicament, and time will determine what happens next'. Leigh's sister Helena described his mood over Christmas 1910 as "extremely sombre." Although he never mentioned football or the fear of being unable to play in the future, she assumed that was at the root of it.

Although Sunderland won their next match against Tottenham Hotspur at Roker Park it wasn't long before the campaign began to disintegrate. The unbeaten record ended the following week away at Middlesbrough. Disappointing 1-1 draws against Preston North End and Notts County allowed the chasing pack to gain further ground on the Wearsiders who eventually surrendered first place on Christmas Eve after a 2-1 home defeat to the new league leaders Manchester United. Robert Allan did his best in goal, but he wasn't Leigh. What's more he didn't inspire confidence in his defenders like the Welshman. The side began leaking careless goals brought about through sloppy individual errors. By the end of January, Sunderland had slipped to fifth.

Whenever possible Leigh continued to watch his team-mates in action whether they were playing at home or away, something that only endeared him even more to the club's supporters especially as he insisted on observing from the terraces instead of sitting in the relative comfort of the grandstand. Only a cynic would suggest he made the effort for financial reasons although Sunderland did continue to pay Leigh's expenses while he was injured, probably as a gesture to ensure he remained loyal to the club until fully fit again.

Late in January 1911 the cast was removed to reveal a painfully thin lower left arm. Leigh began doing gentle exercises and planned on making a comeback before the end of the season in April. However, his impatience would get the better of him. When an invitation arrived to play for the Welsh amateur team against their English counterparts during the final week of February, he decided to risk it and test the strength of the bone. It was a stupid, rash move. The arm survived intact but he didn't play well, Wales sinking to a 5-1 defeat. Despite this he passed himself fit for Wales' Home Nations game against Scotland in Cardiff on 6 March. Aware he was likely to be a weak link, the Scots gave Leigh a torrid time, bombarding him with shots and crosses from just about anywhere inside the Welsh half of the field. It was by all accounts painful to watch, the goalkeeper wincing on several occasions while in the process of catching the ball or being challenged. Wales held out for a 2-2 draw in what would prove to be Leigh's 24th and final international cap. The official excuse given by the Football Association of Wales' selection committee for his absence the following week against England was a shoulder injury picked up versus Scotland. In reality, they simply didn't believe he was up to the job.

The Welsh press – which by now had finally woken up to what football, or 'soccer' as they termed it, had to offer – were, if anything, too easy on Leigh's less than convincing show against Scotland. The *Western Mail*'s correspondent at the game reported that 'Roose kept a brilliant goal and effected some daring saves', adding that 'he was powerless to reach either of the shots that beat him'. Like so many newspapers today, the *Western Mail* had by this time also started assessing each player's individual performance, using words rather than a mark out of five or 10. 'Rough luck, hard lines' was their verdict on Leigh for the Scots game. It is just possible that the paper was guilty of putting journalistic integrity at risk when it came to Leigh in the hope that maybe the goalkeeper might be persuaded to become one of its contributors. If so, then the *Western Mail* wouldn't have been the first to do so. Although the majority of national newspapers stuck to the facts, some regional titles known to be courting Leigh's literary talents were on occasion economical with the truth. Take the *Manchester Chronicle* for example, which described his off-colour performance in the 3-3 draw against Manchester City on 24 October 1910 as 'of the high standard one has come to expect from Leigh Richmond Roose'.

Sure enough word of Leigh's less than inspiring form in a Welsh jersey reached Sunderland who opted to continue alternating Robert Allan with the club's third-choice goalkeeper, William Worrell, throughout March and into April. By that time Sunderland had recovered from their winter blip and begun to string some useful results together. Leigh insisted he was fit but with a full-time job at the opposite end of the country was unable to prove this by attending midweek training sessions. The season drew to a close without him playing a single game for the club since that fateful day at Newcastle in November.

Frustrated at the lack of first team opportunities, Leigh told Bob Kyle that he would be seeking a new team to play for. The news didn't come as a great surprise to anyone connected with Sunderland. A badly broken arm can end a goalkeeper's career today, but in 1911 the chances of recovery were less than 50/50. The parting was an amicable if sad one. Sunderland believed he would no longer be up to the rigours of First Division football, and that in effect his career was over. Leigh respected their decision but thought they were wrong. On the other hand the club and its fans had treated him like royalty for three years. They owed him nothing.

Even so Sunderland once again contacted the FA asking for permission to stage a testimonial game in Leigh's honour. The game would, in the words of a letter sent to English football's governing body, 'be an appropriate tribute to a gentleman who has given so much not just to Sunderland Association Football Club, but the sport in general'. Once more the FA said no on the basis that only professionals could have testimonials, and Leigh wasn't a professional. In theory they had the power to bend the rules, especially for a man who had come to mean so much to various clubs and his country. But the general feeling within the corridors of power seemed to be 'Why should we?' Leigh had refused to co-operate with investigations into his expenses, treated an inquiry into a crowd riot with contempt, and insisted on remaining amateur at a time when the FA was doing its utmost to turn football into a professional sport. In short, he represented everything they despised.

So, as in May 1909, Leigh had to make do with a dinner in his honour instead of a testimonial match. This one was a smaller affair held at a hotel in Newcastle attended by Bob Kyle, the majority of the players, club chairman John Wilson and several directors. The proceeds from an 'unofficial' collection (so as not to breach FA regulations on payments to amateur players) held at the final home game of the season were handed over, together with a silver box inscribed with the words 'From ten cads to a goalkeeper' containing a piece of Roker Park turf.

Before hurrying off to catch an overnight train for King's Cross, Leigh made a short speech promising to "return and irritate every one of you" the following season with another team. It had been a touching send-off, but there was no doubt he meant it.

7

End of an Era

THE telegram arrived postmarked Birmingham during the last week of June 1911, just as Leigh was beginning to think Sunderland might have been right about him never kicking, punching or catching another ball again in anger. It was from Aston Villa Football Club and they wanted him to be their first-choice goalkeeper for the 1911/12 season. There was one proviso – he would have to go to Birmingham to undergo a fitness test. This amounted to little more than a formality with Leigh showing club officials his healed left arm, stopping a few shots and running a couple of laps around a pitch. Job done, Aston Villa told him to return to London and not say a word to anyone about agreeing to play for them.

With the newspapers as usual having concentrated on nothing but cricket throughout the summer months, it wasn't until a fortnight before the season began that the news finally leaked out. People were genuinely surprised, believing the severity of the injury had left him with no alternative but to retire. Second Division Huddersfield

Town even sent two directors to London to try and get him to change his mind, Leigh having played the final five games of the 1910/11 season for the Yorkshire club after it had become clear his days at Sunderland were numbered. He met them over lunch and promised to think about the offer, no more than that. However, someone clearly got their wires crossed because no sooner had Leigh made his debut for Aston Villa than Huddersfield announced they were going to sue the goalkeeper for breach of contract. Leigh responded by asking how they planned on doing this considering he was an amateur who didn't sign contracts. Sure enough the matter died a death – at least for the time being.

Aston Villa believed they had pulled off a major coup by getting Leigh to play for them, even if his reputation as Britain's top goalkeeper had taken a knock in the wake of his rushed comeback from the broken arm. The nation's sports writers clearly agreed. 'Roose is a great capture for the club and he is sure to be popular at Aston', declared the *Athletic News* in its club-by-club preview of the 1911/12 season, adding 'It is unnecessary to dwell on the qualifications of the Welsh international. He is a master of the art of preventing opponents from scoring'. After watching his debut at Bradford City, Tom Baxter of *The Times* wrote 'Aston Villa are lucky to have secured the services of such a keeper. Naturally Roose is short of practice, but his judgement is splendid'.

Even so, Villa suffered a mixed start to the season losing 2-1 to Bradford and 3-0 at home to recently promoted West Bromwich Albion before enjoying successive wins over Arsenal (4-1), Manchester City (6-2) and Everton (3-2). On 30 September Leigh and his new teammates made the short trip across Birmingham to face West Bromwich for the second time in a month. In the 75th minute and with Villa leading 2-1, Albion outside left Benjamin Shearman took a shot that Leigh inexplicably tried to kick clear instead of blocking with his hands. To the amazement of the large crowd he missed the ball completely, gifting the home side the softest of goals and a draw they had barely deserved. 'Roose has no greater admirer than myself, but I should say it was the greatest error he has ever made', wrote 'Harricus' in the *Athletic News*, adding in mitigation that Leigh might have been suffering from mild concussion at the time after colliding with a goalpost while making an earlier save.

Three weeks later Leigh had no excuses to fall back on as Villa crashed 3-2 at home to Sheffield Wednesday. 'It sounds suggestive of sacrilege to say this but Roose on his present form is not the Roose we have been accustomed to see for a number of years, for he seems to have lost his judgement', wrote one correspondent. 'It is true he has not had much assistance from his backs, but on no form that he has shown this year can he be made out to be the original, daring, versatile custodian we once knew'.

The Sheffield Wednesday defeat meant Villa had now conceded more goals than any other team in the First Division, and some spectators took to shouting abuse at Leigh as he left the field. In the sanctuary of the dressing room the goalkeeper sat for a considerable length of time with his head facing the ground. When he eventually looked up, the Villa players were alarmed to see tears in his eyes. In an interview he later gave to *The Times*, outside half Charlie Wallace recalled crossing from his seat, kneeling down to look Leigh in the face, and 'a transparent stare coming back at me, like he wasn't there but in some other place with his mind on some other thing. We all did our best to console him, but I'm not exactly sure how aware of us he was or how much use we were to him'.

Leigh's dip in form coincided with him becoming un-characteristically tetchy away from the football field during the autumn of 1911 with family, friends and even complete strangers all finding themselves on the receiving end of cutting remarks born out of a simmering temper. Occas-ionally these threatened to spill over into something more confrontational, as Helena Roose discovered one afternoon while waiting for a train with her brother at a London station. To kill time Leigh had wandered over to a kiosk on the platform and started browsing through the newspapers on sale. After a few minutes the kiosk owner challenged him to either "buy one or push off." Big mistake. With no more than half a dozen strokes of his right arm a furious Leigh succeeded in sweeping every available newspaper and magazine off the counter and onto the adjacent railway track. Helena remembered being relieved that the owner chose to stand well back rather than try and intervene.

After the personal humiliation of the Sheffield Wednesday game and his post-match tears, few within the corridors of power at Aston Villa were surprised to hear that a telegram from Leigh had arrived saying he didn't feel up to playing in the following Saturday's match at Bury, and that second-choice goalkeeper Brendel Anstey should take his place between the posts. Villa's supposed coup had ended in failure after just two months.

The press came up with various theories for Leigh's loss of form. They included age (fast approaching 34), the poor condition of his damaged arm and even deteriorating eyesight. Remarkably no one bothered to question Leigh's mental state, to ask whether he had lost his bottle as a result of what happened in Newcastle the previous November. In any kind of contact sport there will always be players whose competitive edge gets blunted after suffering a serious injury, one that makes them think twice before putting their neck on the line in the future. Leigh now seemed to have lost that edge. The fearlessness that had always been one of his trademarks had gone.

Ironically Leigh had written a newspaper article three years previously in which he stated there was no place in the game for faint-hearted goalkeepers. It included the lines 'He must not even have a nodding acquaintance with nerves, the bête noire of many a man who otherwise would have been successful. The responsibility which it involves and entails should not have a tendency to make him feel timid, otherwise he must give up the idea of ever excelling'.

After playing just 10 games for Aston Villa during which he conceded by his standards an unacceptable 19 goals, Leigh now faced the dilemma of whether to follow his own advice or try and redeem himself at another club, providing of course there was one out there that wanted him.

As it turned out, there was. And it was much closer to home than any of the clubs he had appeared for over the previous 12 years. Known simply as 'The Arsenal' to their supporters, Woolwich Arsenal played south of the River Thames in Plumstead although plans were already afoot to tap into north London's larger catchment area by moving the club to a brand new site at Highbury, after which the Woolwich half of the name would be dropped. Leigh had developed something of a soft spot for Arsenal having formed good friendships with several of their players on the London social scene. In turn the club had always regarded Leigh highly, manager George Morrell declaring his goalkeeping performance for Sunderland at Plumstead in February 1910 as the finest he had ever seen.

Morrell was aware that Leigh's brief spell at Aston Villa had been an unhappy one, severely denting both his morale and reputation. He hoped that with some familiar faces around him Leigh could regain his confidence and help Arsenal better their highest ever finish of sixth place in 1909. On 16 December 1911 a well above average crowd of around 13,000 converged on Plumstead for his debut against Middlesbrough. The joke afterwards was that Leigh worked harder before kick-off shaking hands with spectators than during the match, so poor were the visitors. What little he had to do in the 3-1 win he did with 'calm assurance' according to *The Times*, only twice venturing out as far as the halfway line to launch attacks (although one long kick of his from just outside Arsenal's penalty area helped set up the third goal). After the final whistle he walked to the centre of the pitch and bowed four times, once to each side of the ground, before clapping the spectators in the main grandstand and mouthing the words 'Thank you' as he left the field.

Leigh's confidence did return over the coming months. He survived a hefty kick to the right hand by a Notts County forward that resulted in a two-week spell on the sidelines. When unavailable, his place went to a Scotsman called Harold Crawford who until the summer of 1911 had been playing junior football for an amateur club in Newcastle called Hebburn Argyle. Leigh came to be regarded by the rookie as something of a mentor, playing the role of goalkeeping coach and even on a couple of occasions giving up his place in the first team so Crawford could gain more experience. 'You couldn't wish for a better education', the young understudy told the *Athletic News*. 'Leigh Roose stands head and shoulders above all others when it comes to goalkeeping and has done for many years.

If you can't learn from him, you can't learn from anyone. He is a master'.

Words of praise, but not strictly true. Perhaps 'was' a master would have been more fitting. Gone were the glaring errors that had blighted Leigh's eight-week stay at Aston Villa, while his mere presence in the Arsenal dressing room inspired those around him. But he was undoubtedly past his prime, conceding the odd goal that the Leigh Roose of old would have had no difficulty keeping out. His kicking – once notorious for its power, range and accuracy – was also proving to be erratic, perhaps explaining his growing reluctance to leave the safety of the penalty area.

If Leigh required any confirmation regarding what people within the game thought of his form, then it came at the beginning of March 1912. When Wales announced their team for the opening Home Nations fixture against Scotland in Edinburgh, it was Robert Evans of Blackburn Rovers who was selected as goalkeeper. The reason given for Leigh's omission by one member of the Football Association of Wales' selection committee was that "he doesn't happen to be perfectly sound at present." Their decision came as a shock not only to the Welsh public but also to the man who for 11 years had, along with Billy Meredith, been the lynchpin of the team. The two keepers were good friends, Evans having played second fiddle to Leigh for over a decade, but it was still a bitter pill to swallow. An era had ended and Evans subsequently kept his place for the following games against Ireland and England.

As if to show the Football Association of Wales what they were missing, Leigh went on to rediscover some of his old form during the final weeks of the season. Appropriately his finest performance came at Sunderland's Roker Park ground on 23 March when he got to fulfil his promise to "return and irritate every one of you" with another team. Given a hero's welcome on arrival at the town's railway station and again before kick-off, he conceded a seventh-minute shot by Harry Low but went on to deny the Wearsiders time and time again with outstanding saves. As the referee brought the game to an end, Leigh took his jersey off and threw it into the crowd before spending at least 20 minutes walking around the perimeter of the pitch shaking hands and talking with spectators. Some, aware of his amateur status but perhaps not of those lucrative expenses claims, tried unsuccessfully to thrust coins into his hands. Leigh liked money but he had morals. With unemployment on the rise in the north-east of England (the region's miners had also recently been on strike over the introduction of controversial new shift patterns) there was no way he was going to accept their hard earned cash.

As the world reverberated to the shock waves sent out by the sinking of the *Titanic* just days earlier, so Arsenal's season came to a close with a home game against Notts County on a warm Good Friday afternoon. Arsenal had nothing to play for whereas the visitors had to win to make sure of staying up. After a period of silence in memory of the victims of the disaster, County tore into the home team with a performance that completely belied their lowly league position. It finished 3-0. Although Leigh made some good saves he was partly at fault for two of County's goals. The final whistle provoked similar scenes to those witnessed at Sunderland the previous month, the finest goalkeeper of his generation walking round the perimeter of the Plumstead pitch talking and exchanging handshakes with spectators. The word 'retirement' wasn't mentioned, but judging by his body language the Prince of Goalkeepers seemed to sense it was all over.

Two months later the FA met for its Annual General Meeting at a hotel in west London. One of the items on the agenda had been put forward by what is known as the Rules Review Committee, a standing committee that considers amendments to the laws of the game and still exists today. For over three years the RRC had wanted to prevent goalkeepers from being able to handle the ball anywhere inside their own half of the field. The issue stemmed from one of Sunderland's fixtures in London which had been attended by two committee members. During the match Leigh had run with the ball as far as the halfway line at every opportunity, bouncing it as he went before launching one of his trademark long kicks or throws. This, the committee members felt, had not only ruined the game as a spectacle by breaking up creative and attacking play but had given Sunderland an unfair advantage, even though Leigh's opposite number would have been free to use exactly the same tactics. The RRC felt something had to be done to curb it. The question was what?

Throughout 1910 and 1911 the RRC members considered various alternatives but were unable to find a solution they all agreed on. Then one of them (the records fail to say exactly who) came up with the blindingly obvious answer of only allowing goalkeepers to handle the ball inside the penalty area. It seemed like the perfect answer involving a minor amendment to what is known as Law 8, which until June 1912 had read:

> 'The goalkeeper may, within his own half of the
> field of play, use his hands,
> but shall not carry the ball'.

The RRC amended this to say:

> 'The goalkeeper may, within his own penalty
> area, use his hands,
> but shall not carry the ball'.

In other words if a goalkeeper wanted to move around his penalty area while handling the ball, he had to bounce rather than carry it as he went.

The amendment still had to be ratified by another committee known as the International Board. However, this was merely a formality, consisting as it did of members from England, Scotland, Ireland and Wales. The AGM passed the rule change which came into immediate effect, and ever since June 1912 goalkeepers have been banned from using their hands outside the penalty area. While it's unlikely that the FA set about changing the laws of the game just to spite Leigh, with whom they appeared to be engaged in an ongoing feud, the amendment to Law 8 did come about as a direct result of his style of play. If there had been no Leigh Roose, then goalkeepers might still be free to handle the ball anywhere inside their own half of the field today.

It may have been a minor amendment on paper but the new ruling was to have major repercussions for goalkeepers and the way they played the game. From the beginning of the 1912/13 season few risked leaving the security of their penalty areas at all, except perhaps for when a ball needed to be hurriedly hacked clear rather than end up at an opponent's feet.

That was the way it stayed for almost 40 years until the arrival on the international scene of a side that would become known as the 'Mighty Magyars'. Managed by Gusztáv Sebes and more often than not captained by the great Ferenc Puskás, Hungary became the darlings of the global game during the 1950s despite never managing to win the World Cup. One 32-match unbeaten run of theirs included 6-3 and 7-1 wins over England at Wembley and in Budapest respectively, the first being dubbed 'the game of the century' by stunned British journalists (it was England's first ever defeat at home to an overseas nation, Ireland excepted).

One of the star performers in Hungary's side throughout the decade was goalkeeper Gyula Grosics who played for the Budapest club Honved. Remarkably similar to Leigh in terms of build and facial features, Grosics (who died in 2014) also liked to push up and act as an extra defender whenever possible. As a result he is widely regarded today as one of the game's pioneers for developing the 'sweeper keeper' style of play. Without wishing to belittle the late Hungarian's achievements, it's more accurate to say he rediscovered it.

Even so, Grosics remained the only one of his kind during the 1950s to adopt the sweeping approach. When he retired in 1962, the practice once again went into hibernation until resurrected 21 years later by Howard Wilkinson, the newly appointed manager of Sheffield Wednesday. Wilkinson employed a tactic that involved launching the ball into the areas on a football pitch known as 'channels', lying roughly 10 to 20 yards in from the touchlines on either flank. The most effective way of doing this was to get his regular goalkeeper, an Englishman by the name of Martin Hodge, to dribble the ball out of the penalty area before kicking it long downfield. Wilkinson believed this method of attack would force defenders into making mistakes or conceding throw-ins from which the ball could be propelled into the opposition's penalty area, creating scoring opportunities.

It wasn't always pretty but proved extremely effective as Wednesday stormed to promotion from the second tier of English football in 1984.

Although only a handful of other sides bothered copying what became known as the 'Wilkinson Way', the sight of goalkeepers dribbling the ball out of their penalty areas soon became increasingly commonplace not just across Britain but also in other parts of the world. By 1990 it had become an accepted practice with managers and coaches encouraging them to do it whenever possible, providing the risk of getting caught in possession was low. Leigh Roose and Gyula Grosics had been acting on initiative. Now goalkeepers were being used en masse as an attacking force rather than just the last line of defence.

Few people, least of all Howard Wilkinson, probably realised it at the time but history had simply started repeating itself.

THE SECOND HALF

WAR AND
PEACE

8

The Fuse is Burning

IT was meant to be a short war, one that according to The Kaiser would be over "before the leaves fall" or at least from a British point of view by Christmas. Those who marched off to fight during the summer of 1914 dreamed of adventure, of becoming heroes in the name of their country. In Berlin, Paris and London the mood was little short of elation with girls bombarding the smiling, departing soldiers with flowers and kisses.

Come December, that mood had quite literally been blown to smithereens. From the North Sea to the Alps, a 500-mile-long gash had been torn across the face of Europe separating the German army from those of Britain and France. For four years home to these soldiers would be a network of muddy trenches in which they lived like rats from day to day. Forget about the glories of war. This was misery on an unimaginable scale.

Initially at least, life back in Britain carried on pretty much as before. Believing that the war would be over in a matter of months, the Football Association had even gone ahead with the 1914/15 season. But as the death toll steadily rose on the Western Front, so attitudes began to change. "This is no time for games," Lord Roberts, one of Britain's most decorated and successful commanders, had told one group of men volunteering to join the Royal Fusiliers. "How very different is your action to that of the men who can still go on with their cricket and football as if the very existence of the country was not at stake." Sure enough, once the season had finished in May 1915 the players went off to the recruitment stations and football was put on hold for the foreseeable future.

Unlike so many of his former teammates, Leigh Roose volunteered immediately to join the war effort. Despite having retired from top flight football in 1912 the game had continued to occupy a large part of his life during the intervening two years. He had played on a freelance basis for various lower league amateur outfits, turning up between the posts in as far-flung destinations as Porthmadog in Wales and Horsham in Sussex (there was even an appearance on the wing for the London Welsh rugby union side as a favour to his brother-in-law who captained the club). These run-outs on what tended to be little more than park pitches frequently led to chaotic scenes with hundreds (sometimes thousands) of people jostling to get a good view of a bona fide sporting superstar. Ever the showman, Leigh made sure every client got their money's worth. He caught shots one-handed, performed acrobatics on crossbars, dribbled the ball out of his penalty area, talked to the crowd, talked to himself. Sometimes he would take out a comb and start brushing his hair mid-match. On other occasions he would stay behind afterwards for 'Beat the Goalkeeper' competitions, inviting spectators to take penalty kicks against him.

It wasn't always football clubs that sought Leigh for his time. Many approaches came from the organisers of events such as fairs and county shows, a game of football being just one of several attractions staged over the course of a day or weekend. As a result Leigh also frequently found himself judging anything from tug of war battles to flower competitions. Far more to his liking was one invitation originating from the Shropshire town of Ludlow to play in a game of football, after which he would announce the winner of a local beauty contest. Never one to miss an opportunity with the opposite sex, Leigh made a pass at the competition's runner-up, a dark haired girl called Elizabeth. They dated for a couple of months until the unfortunate Elizabeth discovered Leigh was still in a long term relationship with another brunette. Unfortunately for Leigh the pair only found out about each other when Elizabeth arrived unannounced at his London apartment one evening to find her rival and boyfriend in bed together. The argument that ensued left Leigh sporting cuts to his face. Which one of his soon to be ex-girlfriends put them there was never established.

Another more financially lucrative sideline was after-dinner speaking. There was no shortage of private members clubs, especially in London, willing to pay handsomely to hear stories about riots at Stoke, fall-outs with the FA and the behind-closed-doors activities of one Matilda Victoria Wood, aka Marie Lloyd. His talks were funny, sometimes crude and fabulously libellous, and by 1913 able to command up to £50 a shot. Multiply that by two or three speeches a week, then add on money earned through his medical career and goalkeeping guest spots around the country, and it's easy to see how Leigh continued to live the high life even after retiring from the upper echelons of the game.

Bust-ups with girlfriends aside, Leigh was also involved in another altogether different type of confrontation around this period, one which ended up spanning over three years. The origins of the dispute dated back to April 1911 and his five appearances for Huddersfield Town – the ones that prompted two of the club's directors to make for London in an attempt to persuade Leigh to join the Yorkshire club rather than Aston Villa. The misunderstanding which resulted from that meeting had seen Huddersfield threaten to sue for breach of contract, Leigh enquiring how they planned to do so when he was an amateur.

On the three occasions when Town had played at home during his brief spell with the club, Leigh took advantage of an open invitation to stay with Hilton Crowther, a wealthy local cotton businessman and one of the club's directors. The two men became friends. However, their relationship soured over the course of 1912 as Leigh unsuccessfully chased Crowther for expenses dating back to his five appearances. When the club went bust at the end of the year Crowther settled outstanding debts with Town's manager, trainer and players from his own pocket but refused to pay his ex-goalkeeper a penny. This only succeeded in angering Leigh even further.

The feud between the pair rumbled on throughout the following year and most of 1914, becoming increasingly bitter as the months passed by. On one occasion Leigh tracked Crowther and his wife down to a London hotel where he allegedly demanded £2,000 – a huge amount for the time – in unpaid expenses before being ejected from the premises for threatening behaviour. He also began bombarding the Crowthers with offensive postcards referring to the family as 'low down dirty thieves', 'dirty Tykes' and 'false windbags'.

"I remember my mother being very upset by all of it," remembered Leigh's nephew Dick Jenkins of the effect that the feud had on Helena Roose. "Leigh actually disappeared for a while around 1913 and she blamed it all on the trouble he was having with the Crowthers. They were very close as brother and sister and she hated seeing him upset. And he really was upset by that."

The whole sorry business reached a climax during November 1914 in a London courtroom, Leigh claiming damages for slander against Crowther who in turn counterclaimed on behalf of himself and his wife for damages for libel. Besides being absent from the proceedings having already enlisted to help with the war effort, Leigh's cause wasn't exactly enhanced by his decision to go legally unrepresented. As a result Crowther's lawyer, Hugh Fraser, had a field day with the floor entirely to himself, portraying the goalkeeper as a greedy, intimidating character who put money ahead of friendship and loyalty. The matter of Leigh's expenses also arose. Why, asked Mr Fraser, would an amateur be entitled to as much as £2,000 when he had no right to receive money in exchange for playing football?

With nobody present to give evidence for the plaintiff, Mr Justice Bray and the jury recorded a verdict in the Crowthers' favour, ordering the absent Leigh to pay £100 plus costs. An injunction was also granted preventing Leigh from continuing to libel the defendants. In the event the fine remained outstanding and Britain paid little attention to reports of the case in the national press. With the country now at war with Germany, it really didn't matter in the grand scheme of things.

Leigh's plan during the late summer of 1914 had been to volunteer to fight for a Welsh regiment. That was until several of his peers in London took the natural step of offering their services to organisations providing medical, logistical and pastoral support to soldiers such as the Red Cross, the Royal Army Medical Corps, the Salvation Army and the Young Men's Christian Association (YMCA). For many years Leigh's family and descendants, not to mention your author, had been under the impression that his war initially began with the Royal Army Medical Corps. However, some excellent detective work by Martin Kender, the Wiltshire-based military historian who sadly died in 2011, revealed that he was in fact part of the YMCA's war effort, joining the organisation in September 1914 and subsequently working in northern France, Malta, the Greek island of Lemnos (a major operations base during the Gallipoli Campaign) and the Egyptian port of Alexandria (another large staging post for Gallipoli).

During the very early days of World War One the YMCA established scores of what were known as 'recreation centres' across the UK designed to provide soldiers on their way to fight with refreshments and perhaps some reading material. The majority of these centres were based at railway stations and other locations through which large numbers of troops were starting to pass. By November 1914 the YMCA had started opening similar centres in key strategic towns and cities throughout northern France plus along vital lines of communication, handing out refreshments to soldiers on the move (one centre based in railway sidings at the port of Étaples reportedly served in excess of 200,000 cups of cocoa every month).

It was at recreation centres like these that Leigh served throughout the remainder of 1914 and all of 1915, working alongside volunteers most of whom were female but including some men largely over military age (he was by now in his late thirties). In the summer of 1915 permission was granted for centres to be established within areas of army operations close to the firing line, providing soldiers with a welcome refuge. By that time Leigh had left France and was moving between Lemnos, Alexandria and Gallipoli where the YMCA had centres, often working alongside staff from the Royal Army Medical Corps (some of whom he knew), so it's easy to see how confusion subsequently arose as to his exact attachment. The latter location in particular would leave a huge, and not altogether welcome, impression on Leigh.

The reasons behind Britain wanting to extend the war as far as the Dardanelles were very simple. Picking a fight against the Turks would open up a second front in the east, leaving the Germans exposed and hopefully breaking the stalemate that existed along the Western Front. The plan went something like this: the Royal Navy would blast its way through the Dardanelles and the Sea of Marmara before anchoring off Constantinople. The mere sight of this awesome armada would be enough to prompt the Turks into revolting, leaving the government with no option but to surrender. This would leave Germany exposed on its Austro-Hungarian flank and the sea lanes to the Black Sea in Allied hands, allowing Russia to be supplied with vital munitions. From there it would be a matter of time before the Russian armies marched into Germany.

There were doubts from the very start, not least among the British admirals whose job it was to begin this chain of events. For starters, ships versus well-fortified forts (overlooking waters containing hundreds of mines) was seen as a bad mismatch. Then there was the underlying fear that the Turkish government wouldn't simply roll over and surrender to the supposed might of the British Empire. As for security surrounding the expedition? Well, there wasn't any. While assembling in Egypt, it seemed every street hawker and shoeshine boy in Alexandria knew Gallipoli to be its destination.

Nevertheless, the fleet (consisting mainly of older boats as the navy didn't want to risk losing its best ships) set sail and began its attack on the morning of 18 March. As had been feared the Turks gave as good as they got. Three British destroyers – HMS *Inflexible*, HMS *Irresistible* and HMS *Ocean* – were put out of action while the French battleship *Bouvet* sank after hitting a mine. The mine-sweepers tasked with clearing the way ahead turned and fled, their civilian crews having no previous experience of working under fire. By sundown almost 700 Allied lives had been lost and not a single mine cleared or gun destroyed. That night the naval bombardment was called off. First blood to the Turks.

Five weeks later, on the morning of 25 April, came the turn of the ground troops. The Allied generals decided to land soldiers on the tip of the Gallipoli Peninsula with the aim of securing the Turkish batteries so the navy could move unopposed through the Dardanelles to Constantinople. The job was expected to take around 72 hours. On three of the five beaches where the British troops landed, resistance was light. The other two provided a taste of things to come with the Turks returning heavy fire from the word go. Thirteen miles up the coast strong currents took the Australia New Zealand Army Corps (ANZACS) past their assigned beach. They landed instead at what would become known as Anzac Cove, pushing inland until coming face to face with the Turkish 19th Division. Under the brilliant command of their leader Mustapha Kemal, the Turks drove the ANZACS back from the central heights of the Peninsula to where they had landed.

From April through until January 1916 the Allies did little but hang on as the battle raged virtually 24 hours a day (it has been said the Gallipoli front never slept). The days brought searing heat, the nights almost unbearable cold. Lice and flies were everywhere as was disease, in particular dysentery. The only way to keep clean was by going for a dip in the sea, accompanied by the threat of being blown to bits by an incoming Turkish shell.

For the YMCA along with other supporting organisations such as the Royal Army Medical Corps, Gallipoli brought with it new dangers. In the past their work had always been regarded as relatively risk free, providing for soldiers away from the front line guns. Not so on the Peninsula where staff were never far from the firing line. The conditions in and around the YMCA's centre, which took the form of a hut, were dreadful. Throughout the 259-day-long campaign Leigh made regular trips by boat between Lemnos, Alexandria and Gallipoli ferrying supplies to ensure that the YMCA centres in all three locations were stocked as best as possible. More often than not his journeys from the Peninsula were made alongside Royal Army Medical Corps staff evacuating injured soldiers to hospitals in Greece and Egypt. His letters home gave some kind of insight into the appalling conditions that he witnessed. 'If ever there was a hell on this occasionally volatile planet then this oppressively hot, dusty, diseased place has to be it', Leigh wrote of Gallipoli during the summer of 1915 to his former Sunderland teammate George Holley. 'If I have seen the fragments of one plucky youth whose body.....or what remains of it…..has been swollen out of all proportion by the sun, I have seen several hundred. The bombardment is relentless to the extent that you become accustomed to its tune, a permanent rat-a-tat-tat complemented by bursting shells. And yet at night the stars are so bright in this largest of skies that one cannot help but be pervaded with a feeling of serenity, peculiar as that appears'.

At the end of 1915 Lord Kitchener arrived from London to appraise the situation with his own eyes. So appalled was he by the overwhelming mood of despondency that he recommended the withdrawal of all Allied forces. The retreat was so impressive that the Turkish troops (themselves also close to breaking point) barely noticed it was happening, the last soldiers being evacuated during the early hours of 9 January 1916. For the Turks, Gallipoli represented a great victory over the most powerful empire in the world at the time. For Australia and New Zealand it continues to play a huge part in the national psyche (both countries mark the anniversary of the Gallipoli landings with what is known as ANZAC Day, commemorating those killed in war and honouring returned servicemen). As for the British, Gallipoli was just the latest in a long line of battlefield fiascos that would occur during the 1914 to 1918 war.

Of the half-a-million Allied troops landed on the Penin-sula throughout the assault, nearly 300,000 were either killed or injured. By the end of January 1916 Leigh's family feared that he might have joined the list of casualties, his regular stream of letters having dried up before Christmas. Enquiries were made, all of which drew a blank. Nobody seemed to know whether he had gone missing before, during or after the evacuation of Gallipoli. As the weeks turned into months and still there was no word, that almost became immaterial. Whatever the circumstances surrounding his apparent death, it seemed as though Leigh wasn't coming back.

The loss of a loved one is, it goes without saying, one of life's tougher trials. It is even harder to accept when there is no funeral to attend or body to bury. Throughout 1916 Leigh's family, in particular his 77-year-old father, struggled to come to terms with their loss. As a pacifist, Richmond Roose had never wanted his son playing any part in the war, a contributory reason behind Leigh's decision to volunteer for the YMCA rather than fight. Now, 20 years after Edward Roose's death from hypothermia, he had lost a second child. Those close to Richmond believed the spark went out of his aging body through believing Leigh to be dead. He would die of natural causes the following year.

With over 760,000 other families caught up in the grieving process, it was years before any kind of normality returned to day-to-day life in Britain. That also applied to sport, with the first post-war Football League season starting in August 1919. Rugby union's Five Nations Championship followed suit in 1920, Wales and England going head to head for the first time since 1914 in Swansea on 17 January.

When the two countries met again at Twickenham almost exactly a year later Leigh's sister Helena Jenkins, together with her husband John (himself injured on the Western Front in 1916 by an exploding mine) and their son Dick, were among those in the crowd cheering on the visitors. Afterwards they adjourned to the Committee Room at the ground for a post-match dinner, a privilege granted to former internationals such as John and their families. Little did they realise their worlds were about to be turned upside down.

"We found we were sitting at a table with Tom Webster, the sports cartoonist for the *Daily Mail* and a very clever man," recalled Dick in 2000. "Tom had known my uncle (Leigh) well. At some point one of us, I can't remember who, said how sad it was about what had happened to Leigh at Gallipoli and how much he would have enjoyed an occasion like this. And straight away Tom said 'No, he didn't go missing at Gallipoli. I played cricket with him in Egypt after the evacuation!' That was the moment we realised he had managed to get out."

This shocking revelation stunned the whole family, especially Helena. It also threw up many questions. Had Leigh perished while travelling back to Britain from Egypt, his ship perhaps torpedoed by a German U-boat? What if he were still alive? Maybe he had suffered some form of breakdown or memory loss causing him to spend the past five years convalescing in a hospital or home? That might explain why he hadn't been in touch.

Over the following weeks Helena and John sent dozens of letters and telegrams to people, organisations and businesses they remembered as having had some kind of link with Leigh. The list included friends, football clubs, hospitals, newspapers, private members clubs, even his favourite restaurants and watering holes. They were desperate to find out (a) if anyone knew where Leigh was, and (b) where and when the last known sighting of him had taken place. Several of those contacted offered to help by making enquiries of their own.

Having been one of the most popular and recognisable sportsmen in pre-war Britain, there was no shortage of replies. The vast majority said they hadn't seen him since around or before 1914. However, there had been sightings during the war. Charlie Buchan, his one-time captain at

Sunderland, had crossed paths with Leigh in northern France and found him to be in "good spirits" (Buchan came through the killing fields of Passchendaele, Cambrai and the Somme without so much as a mark). Richard Sutton, a journalist with *The Times*, also recalled a chance meeting with Leigh in London earlier that summer during which he had mentioned his imminent departure for France.

Then there were those such as George Holley who hadn't seen Leigh during the First World War but had kept up to date with his movements by letter. The postmarks ranged from Bristol to Egypt to the French port of Calais and were dated 1914, 1915 and 1916. From information contained in some of these Helena was able to deduce that he had joined the 9th Royal Fusiliers at some point during the summer of 1916. Holley himself had last heard from Leigh in September of that year at which point the battalion were holed up in trenches around the villages of Agny and Dainville near the city of Arras. After that, nothing.

All the evidence seemed to suggest that Leigh had perished in France at some point during mid-to-late 1916. However, Helena wasn't entirely convinced. Her brother had already come back from the dead once after Gallipoli. She needed to see with her own eyes some kind of proof that he really had gone for good. The Royal Fusiliers, if anyone, would be able to provide it. At least so she thought.

It was now that the search for information regarding Leigh's whereabouts, or perhaps fate, took a bizarre new twist. According to regimental lists, no one with the surname 'Roose' had fought for any battalion of the Royal Fusiliers during the war. Certain a mistake had been made, John Jenkins asked contacts of his both within the regiment and the War Office to check again. All came back with the same answer – nobody called Leigh Roose had ever been a

Royal Fusilier, let alone a soldier in the 9th Battalion. The War Office was also able to confirm that of the four soldiers killed between 1914 and 1918 with the surname Roose, none had been christened Leigh.

The most famous and certainly the most charismatic football player of his generation seemed to have vanished into thin air.

9

The Somme

SO what really happened to Leigh Roose after Gallipoli? Having been evacuated from Gallipoli to Egypt, Leigh returned to London where he decided to sever his ties with the YMCA and do some actual fighting. He attended a recruitment station and joined up as a private in the 9th Battalion of a regiment whose soldiers appeared in almost every significant battle during the whole of the First World War. That regiment's name was the Royal Fusiliers. Which begs another question. Why didn't anyone called Leigh Roose show up on their records?

Perhaps it was a clerical error, a slip of a pen during the recruitment process that was never corrected, or maybe something more sinister. Whatever the reason, on joining the Royal Fusiliers in July 1916 Leigh's surname was misspelled. Instead of 'Roose', it was written down as 'Rouse'.

One wrong letter would prevent Helena and all bar one of his immediate relatives from ever discovering what happened to Leigh. The exception would prove to be his nephew Dick Jenkins, and it would be another eight decades before he learned the truth.

"We did hear some kind of rumour that he'd gone in under an assumed name, but were never able to get to the bottom of it or find out what it might have been," said Dick. "If that had been the case, it might have been because he was in some kind of trouble. What exactly that might have been, I don't know. Perhaps he was trying to hide from something?"

This is unlikely, for two reasons. First, nobody who met or received letters from Leigh around the time of the First World War can recall him being worried about anything other than the war itself. His personal life certainly appeared as carefree as ever. Second, if he was in some kind of bother, then why didn't he go the whole way and adopt a pseudonym?

In all probability the mix-up was caused by nothing more than the slip of an army recruitment officer's pen when it came to one letter, with that second 'o' not quite joining up at the top.

From July 1916 all military correspondence mentioning Leigh spelled his surname 'Rouse'. That included notification of him being awarded the Military Medal for bravery in the attack on Ration Trench at the beginning of August 1916, which received a mention in the *London Gazette* newspaper six weeks later on 21 September. Of course no one who read that report had any idea that 'Private L. Rouse, Regimental Number 10898' was none other than the Prince of Goalkeepers himself.

Unfortunately neither Helena Jenkins nor any of the small army of people searching for information about Leigh's whereabouts ever considered that Private L. Rouse and Leigh Roose may have been one and the same. If they had, then the mystery over his disappearance would almost certainly have been solved straight away.

It has been estimated that 235,476 men fought for the Royal Fusiliers at some point during the First World War, of whom 29,941 lost their lives. Though they came from many different backgrounds some battalions were made up of distinct social groups. For instance the 10th was nicknamed 'The Stockbrokers' consisting as it did of City of London professionals who had joined en masse, while the 18th, 19th and 21st were almost entirely the pride of those who had been to public school or university. Then there was the 23rd and 24th, dubbed the 'sportsman's battalions', full of middle and upper class men who could shoot and ride well.

The 9th, on the other hand, had no such airs or graces. It attracted males from lower middle class and working class professions who had undergone strenuous training in and around the English army towns of Aldershot and Colchester before being sent to France late in May 1915 as part of the 36th Infantry Brigade. By then any hope that this would be a short war had long since evaporated. Come the end of 1915 the total casualty figures for the Allies alone on the Western Front were somewhere in the region of one and a half million, all in return for ridiculously small territorial gains.

As the magnitude of the unfurling disaster became apparent, so morale in the trenches plummeted. The troops began to detest the generals who seemed incapable of coming up with any form of effective strategy, partly due to their cavalry backgrounds (something trench warfare had rendered obsolete) but also because they were out of touch with what was happening on the battlefields (it was said senior officers were rarely seen at the front as the sight of wounded men might affect their judgement when it came to ordering attacks). Where possible the gaps left in the ranks by the dead and injured were plugged by men drafted in from elsewhere. This is how Leigh came to be at the Western Front in July 1916 with the 9th Royal Fusiliers, right in the thick of the bloodiest battle of the entire war.

The main objective behind the Battle of the Somme was to relieve pressure on the French forces caught up to the east at the Battle of Verdun which had been going on since February 1916. It would be a frontal attack through no man's land designed to inflict maximum casualties on the Germans, setting the Allies up for one final push to victory. In charge was General Sir Douglas Haig, commander of the British Expeditionary Force. Besides thousands of men, Haig had new weapons and equipment at his disposal including almost 400 aircraft which had been busy mapping the German trench system. From this the British had constructed a scale model of the enemy's positions to train on beforehand. Detailed maps were also circulated among the regiments with every German trench given an English name for familiarisation purposes. Haig was so confident of success that he promised David Lloyd George, the incoming Secretary of State for War, that he would call off the attack should the casualty figures rise to unacceptable levels.

On 24 June approximately 3,500 Allied guns began pounding an 18-mile-long front stretching north to south between the villages of Gommecourt and Maricourt. The bombardment was designed to last for five days after which Haig seemed to expect the German soldiers – at least those that were still alive – to be begging for mercy. On the fourth day of the barrage it began to rain, resulting in the attack being postponed for 72 hours (throughout which the guns continued to fire). Then at 7.30am on 1 July the order was given for the soldiers to go over the top.

What happened next was little short of catastrophic. The advancing British soldiers, some moving at walking pace as the opposition was expected to be so weak, found their way blocked by barbed wire that was supposed to have been cut. With men still streaming out of the trenches to the rear, a bottleneck soon formed. The majority of those who tried to climb through the wire became trapped and were shot by German troops who had survived the Allied bombardment in their reinforced underground dugouts. To make matters worse for the British, the Germans – alerted by the barrage – had brought up thousands of reserve troops to form a second line of defence. Anyone who did manage to get through found themselves hugely outnumbered.

With communications between the front and command headquarters breaking down those who did survive were left wandering aimlessly in no man's land, uncertain of what to do next. Some estimate that during the first hour of the attack alone as many as 30,000 British soldiers were either killed or wounded. Whatever the truth, the casualty figure had certainly reached around 60,000 by the end of the day, the biggest loss of life ever suffered by the British army in one 24-hour period. Despite this, Haig ordered the attack to continue.

By the time Leigh arrived at the Somme nearly eight weeks later both the Allied and German forces were occupying more or less exactly the same positions as they had on 1 July. The high spirits of June, when the men of the 9th had relaxed by staging cinema shows, concerts and football matches before moving into position ready for the offensive, had disappeared. The presence of one of Britain's most famous sportsmen in the trenches nevertheless provided the soldiers with a welcome distraction. 'Had tea today with none other than Leigh Roose', wrote Second Lieutenant Gerald Bungey in his personal diary. 'An immense and extremely funny man. Told him I had seen him play against The Arsenal in 1910 and that he should have prevented the first goal. With a smile he pretended to draw a pistol and, in effect, shoot me!'

Within weeks of writing this, Bungey would die at the hands of a German sniper.

Leigh was one of many men sent to bolster the ranks of the 9th Battalion towards the end of July. Together they saw their first direct action in operations around the village of Pozieres during the first week of August. On the night of the 3rd, the 8th Battalion Royal Fusiliers had captured a German trench known as Fourth Avenue plus part of another called Fifth Avenue. A decision was subsequently made the following day to stage a further attack that evening on the neighbouring Ration Trench. At just after 3pm on 4 August the 9th moved off to take over parts of the trenches already occupied by the 8th. Though they were spotted and shelled by the Germans, the 9th were in position by 6.30pm with plenty of time to spare ahead of zero hour at 9.15pm. There, both battalions waited for detailed orders to arrive about how the attack would take place.

At 8.15pm they were still waiting and a growing sense of unease was beginning to creep in. The orders finally came with less than 50 minutes to go, far from enough time to adequately brief every soldier. At 9.15pm, accompanied by an intense bombardment, the Fusiliers began their advance, breaking into a charge when 50 yards from Ration Trench. On the left flank things went according to plan. But on the right the attackers stumbled across an unmapped enemy trench, surprising around 100 German soldiers and two officers who immediately opened fire. In the confusion the Fusiliers became separated from each other. It wasn't until late the following afternoon that the hopelessly outnumbered Germans finally surrendered and Ration Trench was taken.

That night the Germans mounted a counter attack on the positions occupied by the 9th. Some of the troops who led the assault were armed with *flammenwerfers*, flamethrowers fired through a smokescreen with the aim of causing as much panic and injury as possible. By all accounts the rookies in the battalion remained remarkably calm and the attack was beaten off with the loss of only 40 yards of trench. It was for his actions during this counter attack that Leigh won the Military Medal. With his clothes burned and struggling to breathe amid jets of burning petrol, Leigh 'continued to throw bombs until his arms gave out and then, joining the covering party, used his rifle with great effect. During the next night, when another attack was expected, he remained close to the barricade'. What this eye witness account, taken from the diary of Sergeant Charles Quinnell, fails to say is that Leigh fought throughout most of the counter attack without a gun, the German advance coming so quickly he had been unable to lay his hands on one in time. Quinnell's words would reach a wider audience when they were included in H C O'Neill's book *The Royal Fusiliers in the Great War*, published in 1922. Yet the author, a respected military historian, still managed to spell Leigh's surname with a 'u' instead of an 'o', perhaps himself unaware of soldier 10898's real identity.

In the weeks that followed the Allies threw everything they could at the enemy in an effort to win the Battle of the Somme. In return, the Germans managed not only to resist the onslaught but to launch further counter attacks. Every battle for every village, farm or woodland meant the loss of more young men. Many of the wounded bled to death where they fell, then lay in the sun for days until becoming a health hazard. Occasionally both sides called truces in order to remove some of the corpses. Those that remained simply sank into the mud when the rains came. And still Haig insisted that the whole sorry business continue.

Contrary to popular belief the troops didn't spend 24 hours a day, seven days a week cooped up in the trenches during the battle. The battalions took turns at manning the front line, allowing those physically and mentally exhausted by their semi-underground existence to get some kind of break. One evening in September some of the 9th witnessed a performance by a concert party at Dainville's YMCA building which, according to a note left inside the battalion's own war diary, 'was greatly appreciated'. Then there were parades to take part in and, less than a week after the attack on Ration Trench, an inspection by none other than King George V, Colonel-in-Chief of the Royal Fusiliers. As irony would have it the King, a keen sports enthusiast, had already come face to face with Leigh. Prior to acceding the throne he had been introduced to the Prince of Goalkeepers before a Wales versus England football international in Nottingham in 1909.

Leigh himself also provided the star turn during another break from the front line by talking to a group of around 200 soldiers about his life and playing career. He opened with one of his regular quips as an after-dinner speaker, designed to emphasise the dangers of goalkeeping – "Before you go to war, say a prayer. Before going to sea, say two prayers. Before marrying, say three prayers. Before deciding to become a goalkeeper, say four prayers." Then, turning the words around, he told the troops that "Under the present circumstances, I think it only appropriate I amend that to before going to sea, say a prayer. Before marrying, say two prayers. Before becoming a Fusilier, say three prayers. Before deciding to become a goalkeeper, say four prayers."

However, the nature of the beast meant that most of the time the 9th were in the danger zone. Some days were quiet, bar the occasional shell, others little short of Armageddon. There were patrols to go out on, snipers and gas attacks to deal with, damaged trench walls to repair and mud – lots of it – especially as summer gave way to autumn. Occasionally something happened to lighten the load. Leigh and Sergeant Quinnell received their Military Medals for bravery at Ration Trench in the dismal surroundings of a trench near Agny. As they were popular figures with their peers this caused for a little celebration courtesy of a bottle of whiskey smuggled in by Lance Corporal Cyril Cross, regarded throughout the 9th as one of the battalion's sharpest shooters. It was while enjoying this little tipple that Leigh was informed he had been promoted from Private to the same rank as Cross. Thankfully, recalled Quinnell in his diary, the rest of the day was 'very quiet'.

As September made way for October, so the weather worsened. Rain fell virtually every day creating, in the words of Major Maurice Coxhead of the 9th, "mud upon mud." Unsurprisingly the sick rate went through the roof. On one particular morning every battalion serving on the Somme as part of the 54th Brigade (which included the 11th Royal Fusiliers) reported between 150 and 250 men as being ill. Having been a goalkeeper Leigh was accustomed to standing around in the rain, but that didn't stop him requiring attention for a mild case of trench foot, a fungal infection brought on by prolonged exposure to damp, cold and unhygienic conditions. At its worst, trench foot could result in gangrene setting in leading to the amputation of toes. Leigh's problems were cured thanks to a new pair of waterproof boots and more frequent changes of socks.

The conditions also began to play havoc with the Allies' overall battle plan. Time and again battalions found themselves going into line ready to launch an attack, only to have their orders cancelled at the last minute due to the appalling weather. The effect this must have had on the men's nerves can only be imagined. At least the generals, criticised for their cocooned existence miles from the front, saw the stupidity in making saturated troops loaded down with ammunition run through ankle deep mud towards hostile fire.

On Thursday 5 October 1916, the 9th together with the 8th Royal Fusiliers (both part of the 36th Infantry Brigade) had been due to lead a major assault on an area stretching between two roads leading north-west and north-east out of Gueudecourt respectively. The Fusiliers were to attack on the left hand flank, with battalions from the 37th Brigade taking care of the right. The first objective was an enemy position known as Bayonet Trench, marked out by a green line on Allied maps, with the second and final objective a brown line called Barley Trench. Zero hour was due to be at 1.45pm but when the day dawned to heavy rain the odds on a postponement were high. Sure enough word came through from Command Headquarters around mid-morning that the attack was off. They would try again in 48 hours' time.

For the next two days the Allies sat tight as shells from both sides passed over their heads. Sometimes the odd one landed too close, killing or severely injuring anyone unfortunate enough to be in the vicinity. At 7.45pm on

6 October the British and French guns stepped up their bombardment to help pave the way for the attack the following day. The Germans, realising something was imminent, did likewise. And so it continued throughout the night until daybreak.

At 9am all Allied watches were synchronised in preparation for the forthcoming advance. Visibility remained fair to good throughout the morning with not a drop of rain falling on the waiting troops. At regular intervals over the next few hours officers moved among the men, issuing advice and instructions. Remember to always move in the right direction, using the sun (if visible) and any other landmark for guidance. Remember to watch out for trenches not marked on the map. Remember Bacon Trench, roughly halfway between the first and second objectives, which once cleared of Germans need not be occupied. Remember that both Bayonet and Barley Trench may have been obliterated and therefore hard to recognise. Remember to watch out for each other, but more importantly look after yourself.

At 1.35pm, the final countdown began.

Unwrap rifle from protective rags and check the thing is clean and ready to fire.

Fix bayonet.

Offer those around you encouragement.

Calm any nerves by being sick.

Say a prayer.

This time, there would be no postponement. Leigh was in the second line of Fusiliers to go over the top. By all accounts he continued advancing even after the man directly in front of him was shot. As the previously unseen German machine guns opened up and more soldiers began falling, it rapidly became a case of every man for himself. Even so, some of those fortunate enough to live another day did remember seeing Leigh out in no man's land. Gordon Hoare, who before the war had represented England as an amateur footballer, spotted him running full pelt towards Bayonet Trench firing as he went.

Sergeant Quinnell, who had been in the first line to go over, saw Leigh lying in a bomb crater although he couldn't be sure if he was dead or taking refuge. Later, when it came to trying to establish who was still alive, a Lance Corporal swore blind he had seen Leigh safe and well back in Allied territory that night. However, the soldier later confessed that with it being dark he wasn't absolutely certain it had been him.

By dusk, everyone connected with the 8th and 9th Royal Fusiliers knew the attack had been a miserable failure. In some areas only stout defending by rearguard troops manning the Allied trenches had prevented the Germans from advancing themselves.

The simple truth was that the creeping barrage hadn't worked. True, the guns had moved with the troops as they ran across no man's land towards the enemy. They just hadn't been very accurate, completely missing the left hand side of Bayonet Trench not to mention other rogue craters containing enemy machine guns.

Hundreds of Fusiliers were either injured or unaccounted for. Some of the wounded had been seen being taken in by the Germans, yet those who survived the carnage knew full well that the vast majority of those still missing were gone for good.

The next morning a message from General Boyd Moss, Commanding Officer of the 36th Infantry Brigade, arrived addressed to the 9th Royal Fusiliers. It read:

'Will you please thank all ranks of your battalion for the magnificent gallantry they displayed yesterday. They advanced steadily under a very heavy fire which only the very best troops could have faced. Although unfortunately unsuccessful, your gallant conduct has added to the fine reputation which you have already won for yourselves'.

The message was by all accounts copied onto scraps of paper and circulated throughout the battalion. Few bothered taking the time to read it.

Besides that one false alarm from a Lance Corporal nobody ever saw Leigh Roose after Bayonet Trench, either dead or alive. He was almost certainly fatally wounded by a German bullet or shell, probably within minutes of the attack being launched at 1.45pm. To this day, his body has never been found. It was either blown to bits or sank into the mud where it still remains.

The Battle of the Somme finally drew to a close five weeks later on 13 November when the rains made way for snow. No breakthrough had been made. For that, Britain suffered around 420,000 casualties and France over 204,000. Nobody knows how many Germans died or were injured, with estimates varying from 437,000 to 680,000.

The killing would continue for another 24 miserable months taking the casualty figures on all sides into several million and wrecking the social and economic fabric of communities across Europe for years to come.

10

The Monument Man

ABOUT an hour and a half's drive south from Calais, along one of the many lanes which meander off the D929 road between Albert and Bapaume, lies the village of Thiepval. Over the course of 88 days during 1916, Thiepval was the focus of some of the bitterest fighting witnessed during the First World War. It had originally been one of the Allies' main objectives on 1 July, the first day of the Somme offensive, but stern German resistance meant it wasn't until 26 September that it was finally captured. As a result, the place was completely obliterated.

Some eight years after the war had ended it was decided that a memorial would be constructed at Thiepval in honour of those soldiers who died at the Somme and whose bodies were never found. It was designed by Sir Edwin Lutyens, probably Britain's best-known architect at the time, and built over the course of four years between 1928 and 1932 (Lutyens was also responsible for the Cenotaph in London's Whitehall). Inscribed on the memorial are the names of over 72,000 'missing' men who belonged to the

United Kingdom and South African forces, soldiers with no known graves from other Commonwealth countries being commemorated elsewhere. 'Overwhelming' is apparently the word most frequently used by visitors to describe Thiepval's effect on the senses, particularly those setting eyes on it for the first time.

Walk across the immaculately kept grass towards the front right hand side of the memorial and you will see Leigh's surname listed in alphabetical order among the ranks of Lance Corporals in the Royal Fusiliers, the initials L R M M standing for 'Leigh Richmond' and 'Military Medal'. It says 'Roose' now. Up until December 2015, to many people's immense frustration, that wasn't the case.

Take away the cemeteries which decorate just about every corner of this beautiful, gently undulating countryside and it is difficult to imagine what happened here in 1916. The battered landscape of splintered trees, shell holes and trenches has been replaced by the very same rural idyll which first welcomed soldiers from both sides here all those years ago, before the guns started firing. Yet scratch below the surface and there are reminders everywhere. Just ask the locals whose cellar walls still bear the carved names of soldiers long dead, or the farmers who continue to turn up body parts while tending to their fields (and, in many cases, bury them again so as so avoid the long drawn out bureaucratic process which accompanies such a discovery). Europe may have changed, but the past refuses to go away.

Gueudecourt lies approximately 10 kilometres east of Thiepval as the crow flies. Nobody seems to know its exact population. It could be anything from 80 to 105, depending on whether or not you include Parisians with weekend homes there. Either way, the figure hasn't changed significantly since the early years of the 20th century. At its heart is a small triangular green which boasts a single set of football goalposts. When the sun shines the older residents come out to sit on the benches surrounding the green and talk, the distant sound of high speed trains travelling between Lille and the French capital occasionally floating in on the breeze.

Drive a couple of hundred yards from the goalposts towards Beaulencourt and you will come to some fields, just before the road begins to climb past the local dairy. On 7 October 1916 this was no man's land across which the Allies launched their unsuccessful assault on German lines. Leigh, together with so many of his colleagues from the 9th Royal Fusiliers, perished in the field immediately on the left which today is used for growing crops. The unkempt bank beyond these fields marked out by long grass and the odd tree marks the line of Bayonet Trench, the Allies' first objective that day.

Try walking 10 yards across these fields in damp conditions and you will understand what Major Maurice Coxhead meant when he spoke of "mud upon mud." Even the slightest of showers is enough to create a clammy mess hell bent on clinging to anything it comes into contact with, the same clammy mess soldiers from both sides had to put up with for weeks on end. If you have ever wondered how a dead body can just sink without trace into the ground, then this small corner of France on a wet day will satisfy your morbid curiosity.

In the nearby cemetery at Flers, home now to so many of Leigh's regiment, there is one grave dedicated to 'A Solider of the Great War' from the Royal Fusiliers who died on either 7 or 8 October 1916. Whoever it was would have been identified by his uniform, there being very little remaining of the body that was once inside it. Perhaps this spot marks the final resting place for the Prince of Goalkeepers, perhaps not. But for those who care anything about Leigh, it – along with the towering Thiepval Memorial – is about as personal as it gets.

It has been estimated that around 702,400 servicemen from the United Kingdom alone were killed or went missing in the First World War. Among them were several well-known footballers Leigh counted as friends including Sunderland left back Albert Milton, mortally wounded while fighting for the Royal Field Artillery on 11 October 1917, centre forward Wilf Toman of Everton, killed in action on 2 May 1917 while fighting for the King's Liverpool Regiment, and Seaforth Highlander Peter Johnstone, one of seven Celtic players to die in the war, killed at the Battle of Arras in May 1917. Like Leigh, Johnstone's body was never recovered.

Under normal circumstances their deaths would have led to widespread mourning within the communities served by their respective clubs. But these weren't normal circumstances. Though the passing of all three warranted mentions in newspapers across northern England and Scotland, the sheer scale of what was happening in France meant the average supporter simply didn't have the time or emotional capacity to grieve properly for them. Why mourn a football player when your father, brother, uncle or cousin wasn't coming home?

At least Milton, Toman and Johnstone's deaths were documented, no matter how briefly. Leigh wasn't so fortunate, which is hardly surprising considering he had been serving under the wrong name in a country few outside his battalion knew he was in – one on the other side of Europe from where his family had erroneously been told he was missing presumed dead. Unlike Johnstone at Arras, nobody actually witnessed his last breath. Small wonder that even the most avid Stoke or Sunderland supporter remained oblivious to Leigh's fate. Having already retired from top class competition two years before the outbreak of war, it wasn't as though his absence was especially felt when league football resumed in August 1919. People just assumed he had got on with his life away from the sport.

That isn't to say Leigh was forgotten, at least not initially. He had been a hero to many thousands of people in all corners of England and Wales, and continued to be so for years to come as Dick Jenkins discovered through a chance encounter just after the Second World War.

"When I came back from Burma where I had been serving, I was posted to the Senior Medical Office at a place called Tern Hill in Shropshire," recalled Jenkins. "Once there I discovered that my Physical Training Sergeant was a man called Frank Soo who was part Chinese, part English and played inside forward for Stoke. Before he went off for one game, I said to him that my uncle had also played for Stoke as an amateur before World War One. And straight off Frank said 'L R Roose', just like that. He said his photograph was still hanging in the directors' room and that he was regarded as one of the greatest players ever to have played for the club."

Yet as the years passed so Leigh's light began to fade, dimmed by the chill winds of another world war costing the lives of at least 295,000 United Kingdom forces personnel not to mention around 60,600 civilians. The bombing of Ministry of Defence offices in Southwark during the London blitz of 1940/41 destroyed 60 per cent of all personal First World War diaries kept by British soldiers. Leigh's was among that number, preventing future generations from discovering more about him (providing of course they would have known to look under the surname 'Rouse'). As with so many other great football heroes from the pre-*Match of the Day* and Sky TV eras very little of his star pedigree was captured on film for posterity, with only Sagar Mitchell and James Kenyon's footage from the Wales versus Ireland game of 1906 surviving into the 21st century.

The nature of Leigh's death also did his legacy few favours. No body equals no grave. Until as recently as 2015 the only ceremonial mention of Leigh's sacrifice for King and country carrying the correct spelling of his name could be found on a wall inside Holt Presbyterian Church where he was listed as one of 11 local men to have lost their lives in the First World War.

All things considered it was just as well word of mouth still counted for something, otherwise the pioneering role and outstanding achievements of one of the game's great characters might have been lost forever.

"There was always talk of this amazing guy back in the 1960s when I was a fairly young chap," says the Welsh football historian Gil Jones. "I remember hearing it and thinking 'Wow, what a remarkable man'. But it wasn't until Geraint Jenkins, who had also heard all the stories, wrote about Leigh in his book on the giants of Welsh football that I really began to sit up and take notice. I'd been over to the Somme several times and passed the trench where he won his Military Medal without realising it. That's when it really began for me."

The 'it' in question was a campaign started during the 1990s by various Welsh football enthusiasts and historians including Gil Jones and Geraint Jenkins to perpetuate Leigh's memory, specifically by persuading the Commonwealth War Graves Commission (which maintains the graves and commemorative locations of

Commonwealth military service personnel who died in the two World Wars) to change the spelling of his name on the Thiepval Memorial from 'Leigh Rouse' to 'Leigh Roose'. "It shouldn't be a big deal," Jones said back in 2002. "I've been to Thiepval several times and seen Commonwealth War Graves workers changing names, even deleting names because they do find (the remains of) some of these people. Not many, I grant you, but they can make amendments to that memorial."

Despite the sending of many letters and documents to the CWGC including copies of Leigh's birth certificate, it was a campaign that for many years fell tantalisingly short of its objective. The CWGC stated that it needed 'documentary evidence connecting the birth certificate with the casualty'. Yet that proved nigh on impossible. In census forms, football match reports, letters, history books and regimental diaries he was referred to as either 'Leigh Roose' or 'Leigh Rouse'. Not one scrap of paper existed which categorically stated they were in fact one and the same. If the war diary of the 9th Royal Fusiliers (in which he is referred to as 'Rouse') had at some point mentioned his football background then that would probably have satisfied the CWGC. But it didn't. Similarly none of the surviving letters sent by Leigh during the war to friends such as George Holley bore the name Leigh Roose. All were simply signed 'Leigh' or carried a humorous pseudonym such as 'The Archdeacon'.

As for obituaries dating back to 1916 which the CWGC said would suffice as evidence, providing they mentioned his football career and military service? Well there weren't any because none were written in the first place, a consequence of so few people knowing he was in France and his family already believing him to be dead.

A stalemate had been reached which, much like the hostilities out in France during World War One, would take years to break. Speaking again in 2002, Jones added, "It has been frustrating but I, we, will continue because this man deserves to be remembered. He was a war hero, as well as a hero on the field of play. He won the Military Medal in action on the front line, yet you try and check his name on the war graves register and you can't find it. That's not right. It's high time he came in from the cold. You know, I can just see him when he won his Military Medal at Ration Trench, or when they were attacking Bayonet Trench, in that he was probably behaving exactly as he did on the playing field for Stoke City, Sunderland or any of the other teams he played for. It was almost a game, although of course it wasn't against Newcastle United or Liverpool. It was against the Bosch. There are parallels there. Leigh wasn't the kind of guy who would have stood in a crowd. He was a leader, and that ultimately may have been his undoing."

As Leigh himself once wrote, 'If a thing is worth doing at all, it is worth doing properly and with all one's energy, and he who gives hard knocks must be prepared to accept hard knocks in return'. It was a maxim Leigh applied to all aspects of his life, not just football. And that included war.

Although word of mouth undoubtedly prolonged Leigh's legacy, especially in his native Wales, it also helped fuel several untruths. Take, for instance, the romantic but completely erroneous story about him playing football against German soldiers amid the bomb craters of no man's land on Christmas Day 1914, when in fact he was well away from the front line with the YMCA. Another falsehood perpetuated down the years was that he joined the Royal Welsh Fusiliers following his decision to leave the YMCA, an easy slip to make owing to Leigh's place of birth. Similarly, others assumed that he enlisted in one of the Royal Fusiliers' sportsman's battalions simply because he played football, when in fact these tended to cater for middle and upper class men who specialised in country pursuits such as shooting. "Stories get repeated over the years from person to person and somewhere along the line bits get changed," says Geraint Jenkins. "The result is of course that sometimes it becomes increasingly difficult to separate what is fact from what is fiction."

Helena and John Jenkins separated in 1930 after which she began a new life in the English south coast resort of Bournemouth. Yet Leigh's fate, and one incident in particular, continued to haunt her. After war was declared in 1914, John Jenkins had moved his family from London to the relative safety of Swansea where they remained until hostilities ceased four years later. Although Helena wrote to Leigh informing him of their change of address, she later discovered that he had visited their old house in Highgate around June 1916 only to find it empty. The two were destined never to lay eyes on each other again.

It was this melancholy image that fired Helena's ceaseless quest to discover what exactly had happened to Leigh, one that would last the rest of her life. Countless letters were written and personal visits made to anyone she believed might hold a piece of the jigsaw. She lobbied her local Member of Parliament, went for meetings at the French Embassy in London and even contacted national newspapers based in Paris. To her dismay, every turning led to a dead end.

In her brother's absence, Helena also became obsessed with learning more about Leigh's life from some of those who had known him best, including old friends from the football world. George Holley remembered her visiting his home in Wolverhampton on at least three occasions and delighting in hearing stories about their exploits together while playing for Sunderland. Billy Meredith, who knew Leigh better than just about anybody inside or outside the sport, not only helped fill in some of the blanks but became a close friend, the two exchanging Christmas cards right up until 1957, the year before his death.

Helena passed away in 1966 without ever finding out what became of her brother. "Knowing what I know now, I'm quite glad that she didn't," said Dick Jenkins, her son, when I first interviewed him in 2000. "I lived and fought through a world war, but I didn't have to put up with the physical discomfort that those chaps did in France. My God, what an awful war. What an awful thing for those people to have to go through. I would far rather my mother remember him in happier times, like when he would take us all for lunch at Scott's in Piccadilly dressed in his morning coat and hat, really quite the man about town. That's the sort of memory I hold dear."

It was a sentiment shared by Nick Jenkins, Dick's son. "There were always a lot of questions about what happened to him in France. Now we have answers to those questions, which we are eternally grateful for. But that doesn't escape the fact that he died a quite horrible death in horrible circumstances. There was no body – that says it all really. I'm delighted that my father, right at the end of his life, has finally discovered the truth. But would it have been of any real benefit to Helena? I'm not so sure."

For many years all that remained as far as Leigh's family and descendants were concerned was for the Commonwealth War Graves Commission to see sense and, in Nick's words, "do the right thing" by changing the spelling of his name on the Thiepval Memorial. "What happened to Leigh was a great mystery," said Nick in 2005. "He was meant to have been lost at Gallipoli. As it turns out, he died in France. We know that now beyond all doubt. Changing the spelling of his surname to what it's meant to be would be a fitting end to the mystery. It's something that could be done. It's something that should be done."

In December 2006, the CWGC finally blinked. Roy Hemington, the Commission's records manager, had waded through the mounting pile of evidence and decided that Leigh Rouse and Leigh Roose could only be the same person. Overnight, the spelling of Leigh's name changed on all electronic records held by the Commission. Visitors to the CWGC's website found that Lance Corporal Leigh Rouse, Military Medal, 9th Battalion Royal Fusiliers had become Lance Corporal Leigh Roose, Military Medal, 9th Battalion Royal Fusiliers. Under 'Additional Information' (and alongside a range of other facts such as his service number, date of birth and age at the time of death) it stated he was a former football player who appeared for Wales and served in the war as Leigh Rouse. The stalemate had at last been broken.

But there was a catch. The CWGC declared that it would only change the spelling of Leigh's name on the Thiepval Memorial when the individual panel on which it was inscribed needed replacing. That might be in five, 10 or even 20 years, but was always more likely to be later rather than sooner as the panel was in a relatively good condition. "We don't just tend to send people up the memorial with a chisel," said a Commission spokesman at the time. "That would look unsightly. We operate a panel replacement scheme so that when one panel becomes particularly worn or weathered, we change it. When the time comes to replace that particular panel, then the new one will carry the correct spelling of his name."

This form of protocol, while understandable, nevertheless came as a massive blow to those who had campaigned so long for Leigh's name to be changed. Some were in what might be called their autumn years. If it was going to be decades, then they wouldn't be alive to see it. Responding in December 2006 to the CWGC's decision, Ian Garland said, "I'm delighted that the Commonwealth War Graves Commission has at last agreed to amend its records on Leigh, the most colourful character to play football during the Edwardian era and one of four Welsh soccer internationals to die during World War One, but I've got to say I'm extremely disappointed that nothing looks like being changed on the Thiepval Memorial for many years to come. I can see the Commission's point of view, especially as cash is probably at a premium, but surely there's some way around it? You know, get a group of people together to contribute because Leigh has so many admirers out there who want to do justice to his memory. I think that's something that might be looked into now."

Fast forward to 2015. Just when the idea of some kind of group contribution appeared to be coming to fruition, so the Department for Culture, Media and Sport announced that it would be providing £1.6 million for the 'restoration and enhancement' of the Thiepval Memorial as part of the UK government's programme to mark the centenary of World War One. If cash had been at a premium beforehand, then it certainly wasn't now. Some gentle reminders about Leigh Roose duly went whistling through cyberspace in the direction of Maidenhead, Berkshire, headquarters of the CWGC. During the first week of December 2015 a stonemason set to work removing Leigh Rouse – someone who had never existed anyway – from the Thiepval Memorial, and at long last Leigh Roose took his rightful place among the ranks of his missing comrades.

"The difficulty we had in correcting the name was that much of the official documentation spelt Leigh's name as we had originally engraved it upon the memorial," said the CWGC's media and marketing manager Peter Francis who, it should be said, deserves credit for keeping abreast of the Leigh Roose story and bringing those cyberspace messages to the attention of his superiors. "As such, we had to treat the name as an alias. Men enlisted under different names for all sorts of reasons during the war. Some were even discharged and then managed to re-enlist using a false identity. Although we may never know why Leigh's name was spelt as it was – a simple clerical error or not – it made changing the name more complex from both an evidential point of view and a practical one, there not being enough room on the memorial to list both names together as is our normal practice. Given the evidence supplied the CWGC decided to change the name on the panel, to list Leigh's awards and initials, and then add the 'alias' when that panel eventually comes up for replacement. With the 100th anniversary of the Battle of the Somme in 2016, it is fit and proper that Leigh's name is now engraved as it should be. I have no doubt that visitors to the memorial in years to come will look for his name, be inspired by his deeds and remember him and all those who died."

Sadly the change came too late for Dick Jenkins who died in 2008 just short of what would have been his 103rd birthday, severing that last link to his uncle in terms of people who had actually met or known Leigh. "That's a shame, it really is, but the main thing is that it's finally happened," said Nick Jenkins. "It's good that people who know about Leigh will be able to go there for years to come and see the right name. It's taken a while, far too long if I'm honest, but it's still brilliant news."

"Leigh was a remarkable man in a remarkable number of ways," Dick Jenkins had said shortly before his own centenary. "As a sportsman we are unlikely to see his kind again, and not just because he played as an amateur. He fought for his country and gave his life, yet there is no record of him on any memorial. It would be splendid if that could be changed, even if it's not in my lifetime. You know, I had no idea he had even made it to the Somme, fighting within walking distance of my father (John Jenkins) as it turned out. The only difference was that my father was a Colonel and Leigh was a Lance Corporal. That, and my father came home."

The CWGC's prolonged and arguably overzealous stance regarding Leigh contrasted sharply with that of the Wales Screen Commission, the body set up in 2002 to promote the concept of Wales being a film-friendly nation (and now known as Wales Screen). Towards the end of 2005, the Commission decided it wanted to unveil a plaque at the Racecourse Ground in Wrexham to commemorate Sagar Mitchell and James Kenyon's film of the Wales versus Ireland game from almost a century earlier, the one believed to be the oldest footage anywhere in existence of an international football match. The player chosen by the Commission to have his face featured on the circular plaque was Leigh, partly due to him having grown up just outside Wrexham but also – in the words inscribed on the plaque – because he was a 'football and social phenomenon, not only an excellent goalie but also a national famous playboy'.

The plaque was unveiled by the former Liverpool and Wales striker John Toshack MBE on the afternoon of 2 April 2006, 100 years to the day after Mitchell and Kenyon had shot their historic film. To mark the occasion a recreation of the Wales versus Ireland match took place involving pupils from a local secondary school, the boys involved having spent the previous fortnight learning how to play according to the rules circa 1906. The part of Leigh Roose in the Welsh goal went to 15-year-old Matthew Geddes, goalkeeper for the Year 10 side at Saint Joseph's High School. For the record the match once again finished all square, this time at 1-1 rather than 4-4.

While the game took place talk among the invited guests turned to which goalkeepers of more recent times most resembled Leigh Roose, not just in terms of skill but also personality. Some suggested the former Liverpool player Bruce Grobbelaar, a veteran of the Rhodesian National Guard whose excellence between the posts was occasionally punctuated by the odd howler of a mistake. Having also appeared for Everton and represented Wales with distinction, Neville Southall was perhaps a more obvious if highly appropriate choice. Then there was the former Manchester United and Denmark goalkeeper Peter Schmeichel, a tremendously skilful player with an immense throw who, like Leigh, managed to raise the goalkeeping bar in terms of ability, athleticism and competitiveness. Despite the differences in opinion, all were agreed on one thing. If it hadn't been for Leigh Roose and his pioneering role in the evolution of goalkeeping then Bruce, Neville and Peter might never have been inspired to play the game in the first place.

The plaque's reminder that Leigh had been a 'nationally famous playboy' also provoked its fair share of debate among those present at the unveiling. How many women did he actually sleep with? Answer: it's impossible to say.

Why did he never marry? Answer: he never seemed to meet the right person and according to friends and family wasn't the marrying kind. Did any of his affairs produce children? Answer: none that we know about. In 2006 a man called Nicolas Roose living in the Belgian city of Ghent contacted the BBC website wanting to know if Leigh might be his great-grandfather, his own grandfather having been born an orphan in 1915. The lack of documentary evidence regarding the circumstances surrounding the child's birth and subsequent adoption means we will probably never know. It's possible, but highly unlikely.

Besides honouring a small part played by a deceased relative in celluloid history, the Commission's decision to commemorate the 1906 Wales versus Ireland game also had unexpected consequences for some people with blood links to Leigh Roose. In the months leading up to the ceremony, newspapers and radio stations covering north Wales and areas along the Welsh/English border ran appeals to track down relatives of the players so they could be invited to the event. Some 90 years after Leigh's death, several people were to discover that they had slightly more in common with each other than simply being Welsh or having Welsh ancestry.

"I'd first heard all about Leigh from my father when I was a small child," said Olwen Roose Jones of Wallasey on the Wirral who read about the appeal in her local paper the *Daily Post*. "My grandfather had been a first cousin of Leigh's and my father remembered him coming to our house in Wallasey to see my grandfather. After he told me about him, I went away and read some more in a Welsh 'Who's Who' book that we had.* That's how I came to understand that he had been one of the greatest football players of his generation. Anyway, I wrote in to the *Daily Post* saying that I was a distant relative, explaining the link and asking if that was close enough. It obviously was because I got a phone call within days inviting me along. I knew years ago that Helena's son was a doctor living in Shrewsbury but I'd never had any contact with him. I didn't even know if he was still alive. By responding to that newspaper appeal, I found out that not only was he still alive but that he also had two sons who knew all about Leigh."

Unfortunately Helena's son, Dick Jenkins, was 101 years old at the time and too frail to make the round trip from Shrewsbury to Wrexham for the ceremony to mark the unveiling of the plaque. However, one of his two sons, David Jenkins, was able to join Olwen at the Racecourse Ground to witness the event. "It was a wonderful day in every sense of the word," added Olwen. "I got to meet David, the weather was beautiful and the organisers had arranged for footage of the game to be shown on a continuous loop throughout the afternoon. I know it's only two or three minutes long but it was amazing to actually get to see him play, to understand something about why he was regarded so highly."

(*It is likely that the 'Who's Who' book referred to by Olwen Roose Jones was the *Dictionary of Welsh Biography* published in 1959 by the Honourable Society of Cymmrodorion, an organisation established to promote literature, the arts and science in Wales. The book took 22 years to write and spans 1,157 pages, the majority of them rammed with obscure Baptist and Methodist preachers and ministers. Although the Society deemed Leigh's life worthy of half a page there is no mention whatsoever of his close friend and fellow Welsh international Billy Meredith, considered by some to be the finest player ever to wear his country's shirt. Then again Billy, unlike Leigh, wasn't born the son of a Presbyterian minister.)

Living some 150 miles south-east of Wrexham in the English county of Bedfordshire, Gaynor Tinsdale remained oblivious to the search for relatives of players from the 1906 game. Her grandfather had been John Stevens Roose, Leigh's brother, who died before Gaynor and her twin sister Maggie were born. However, she remembered visiting Helena Roose – 'Auntie Lena' – in Bournemouth as a child and had even come to inherit a pearl necklace that once belonged to her. Gaynor knew her late great-uncle had been a Welsh international footballer, but there it ended. Until 2015 that is, when word reached her about something that was happening in Holt, the Roose family's spiritual home.

For several years Holt resident Brian Payne had been pondering the idea of getting Leigh's name added to the village's war memorial (being a London resident on the outbreak of World War One, Leigh wasn't considered prior to its dedication in 1920). In 2015, with the 100th anniversary of both the Battle of the Somme and Leigh's death rapidly approaching, Brian decided to act. He raised the matter with Holt Town Trust which had no objections, but suggested he should canvass the village for opinion.

"So I did," said Brian. "I put a note through every door with a brief summary of Leigh's life and asked people to let me know if they supported it or disagreed. And I got 165 replies, all of them in favour. If there was anyone out there who wasn't, then I didn't hear from them. That's a pretty good response from a village Holt's size, if I'm honest. I'd already been in touch with Wrexham Borough Council and also the War Memorials Trust to get advice because I thought there might be rules about putting inscriptions on war memorials, but apparently every village has its own set of rules. I tried to find out what the rules were for Holt but the Town Trust minutes for the period around the First

World War were missing. So I went to Wrexham to ask for permission and also had to get support from Cadw which is the Welsh equivalent of English Heritage. I thought it might take two years or 18 months at best to get a reply. In my mind I was thinking 'If I can get it by the centenary of his death, then that would be good'. And in fact it only took a couple of months before they came back saying yes, so I got it a year early!"

A few weeks prior to Remembrance Sunday 2015 the name 'Leigh Roose' was inscribed onto Holt's War Memorial, situated no more than the length of a football pitch from The Manse. And on Remembrance Sunday itself in November an emotional Gaynor Tinsdale, accompanied by her husband Barry, not to mention a good proportion of Holt's population, was there to hear it being read out by the presiding minister who also said a few words about Leigh together with Brian Payne's sterling efforts to perpetuate his memory.

"We stayed there for the weekend and the whole thing was so inspiring," said Gaynor. "I had known that my great-uncle was a goalkeeper, and that was about it. My father was over 40 when my sister and me were born and he died just before I turned 40 at a time when I was living with two young children and trying to hold a job down. My mother had died when we were just 11 and she was 36. I always think it is mothers who in many ways keep families together, because fathers don't talk about lots of things. My father was a wonderful father, but in those days being over 40 seemed really old. Overnight he became more of a grandfatherly figure stuck with a pair of twin daughters. He'd had two heart attacks over the previous years so he was meant to be the ill one in the family, not my mother. As a result I feel like I missed out on a lot of things, like those family stories that get passed down through the generations. I didn't get that. There wasn't a lot of talk of who was who and where and when. So suddenly I'm going from knowing that my great-uncle was a goalkeeper to discovering that he was this incredible figure who played for all these top clubs and was also a war hero. It felt very strange, a peculiar mix of sadness and yet elation because I was discovering so much about my family past. I've been to Thiepval and yet I never knew he was remembered there. You go to Thiepval, and you see the names that are on Holt War Memorial and hundreds of others like it, and you think 'I hadn't even left university by the time they gave their lives'. I know Leigh was quite a bit older when he died, but most of them were barely kids. It makes you very humble."

"It was an emotional day," added Brian Payne of Remembrance Sunday 2015. "It was lovely to have Gaynor and her husband here and indeed Nick Jenkins, Leigh's great-nephew, who was unable to make it on the Sunday but who came up to Holt from Shrewsbury the day beforehand. I'm glad we had that time together and for them to see Leigh's name on our memorial. That's when you think 'Yes, this has all been worthwhile'. It sort of feels as if Leigh has finally come home."

11

Leigh's Legacy

THE laws that govern their position may have occasionally changed together with the colour of the shirts they wear, yet the goalkeepers' lot remains a remarkably similar one to when a young Leigh Richmond Roose first decided to take up the last line of defence on a football pitch. Just as it was back in the late 19th century at Holt Academy, so the tallest boy in the school still tends to end up between the goalposts or jumpers in the playground (and I'm sorry ladies, but even in these enlightened times you still rarely find a girl keeping goal in a school kick-around). He might pull off eight or nine excellent saves yet be mocked for days because of the 'easy' one that got away. He will be the butt of many jokes challenging his ability or sanity, sometimes both. Heard the one about the suicidal Scottish goalkeeper? Threw himself in front of a bus – and the bus went under him.

It doesn't always get much better for those goalkeepers fortunate enough to make a steady or decent living from the game. Goalkeepers command fewer newspaper column inches and less TV time than, say, centre forwards. That's because centre forwards score goals, goals are sexy, and sexy sells.

Saves, someone somewhere has deemed, aren't sexy. Centre forwards, not to mention most outfield players, are likely to be on better wages than goalkeepers. They will be transferred between clubs for higher fees. They will get the pick of the groupies who swarm around footballers. That, unfortunately, is the way it is.

Yet deep down just about anyone with an affinity for the game knows a football team is nothing without a good goalkeeper. A good goalkeeper inspires those in front of him to play with confidence and composure. A good goalkeeper can be worth anything between 10 and 20 points a season, maybe more. A good goalkeeper is likely to be the first name on a manager's team sheet. A good goalkeeper is where a new manager starts with his team rebuilding programme, following the tried and tested method that you start at the back and work your way forward. A good goalkeeper is, in short, a gem.

Leigh Roose was there at the birth of this grudging respect for the art of goalkeeping. So too were men like William Foulke, an ex-miner whose outstanding form for Sheffield United and England wasn't matched by his dietary habits, a combination of cirrhosis of the liver and excessive weight leading to his premature death aged just 42. Others present include the Scot Henry Rennie (more commonly known as Harry), another who enjoyed coming out of goal whenever possible to act as an extra defender, Leigh's predecessor at Sunderland Ned Doig, and James McAulay of Dumbarton who switched from centre forward to keeper believing he could hardly do a worse job than the club's regular number one.

Leigh, however, was in a different league altogether. Not only was he an outstanding goalkeeper but his profile was greater than that of any centre forward during the inaugural decade of the 20th century. He was so good at what he did that the Football Association changed the laws of the game just to keep him in check. His lavish expenses claims meant he was richer than the vast majority of players, despite being an amateur. Editors wanted him for his way with words. Women wanted him for his charm and good looks. He was, by today's standards, an 'A' list celebrity. That didn't happen to goalkeepers then. That doesn't tend to happen to goalkeepers now.

On paper football as an industry in England and Wales has never been healthier. The Premier League is the most popular of its kind in the world with television money generating staggering wealth among players in the game's upper echelons. Yet underneath there's considerable discontent among traditional fans increasingly priced out of watching football who remember the days, not so long ago, when players lived among them and not in gated communities. They resent sections of the media for conning the wider public into believing football only really began in 1992 with the arrival of the Premier League, and anything that occurred beforehand doesn't really count. This discontent has given birth to a burgeoning retro movement consisting of fans who are going back in time for their regular fix of football entertainment. Groups such as the Everton Football Club Heritage Society, which actively promotes the history of the club since its formation, are flourishing as are other mediums such as the magazine *Backpass* dedicated to football in Britain up until 1992. It's not simply a case of grumpy old men sitting around moaning about how things were better in their era – an era that was, after all, riddled with hooliganism and widespread racism. It's just that many supporters are fed up with the greed, corporatism and marketing spiel that has been allowed to run riot through the domestic game. And as they delve back through the history books in search of when football, for all its faults, had a soul, so fans are discovering and identifying with pioneering characters such as Leigh Roose.

"We need to remember what has gone before, and make sure that future generations of football supporters do likewise," says Paul Wharton, chairman of the Everton Football Club Heritage Society (which in conjunction with the Everton Shareholders Association unveiled a plaque outside Goodison Park in 2014 dedicated to the club's seven ex-players who perished in the two World Wars). "I'm an Evertonian and I travel home and away supporting the current team, but I'm proud to be part of a group that's devoted to the history and traditions of Everton Football Club right back to the days of Leigh Roose and beyond. So much about the modern day game disgusts me, and I know I'm far from alone in feeling that way. The people who run football today wouldn't be where they are now without the players and supporters of previous generations. Granted, Leigh could be a controversial figure, but he also had the common touch with all fans, mixing freely with the football public which is something that the pampered modern footballer won't do. Like Neville Southall, another great Welsh Evertonian who also happens to be our Society's patron, Leigh was a true goalkeeping giant who will never be forgotten."

From his vantage point as Sunderland's club historian and match programme editor, Rob Mason is similarly well placed to ensure that Leigh's contribution to the cause on the banks of the River Wear continues to be celebrated. "L

R Roose is a legendary figure at Sunderland, just as he is at his other clubs," says Rob. "Having punched a Sunderland supporter unconscious on a visit as a Stoke player before he ever played for the Wearsiders, no one would have been in any doubt that Roose was a man to look out for when he arrived at the club. At the time Sunderland's crowd was made up predominantly of pitmen and shipyard workers, so they wouldn't have had any qualms about Roose knocking someone out. Supporters like players who match their own passion. It's true that different clubs seem to have specific positions that become special. For instance, at Manchester United the number seven shirt has become iconic. Up the road from us, Newcastle United idolise their centre forwards. At Sunderland, it's goalkeepers who rule the roost. Jim Montgomery is world famous for making Wembley's greatest save in the 1973 FA Cup final but Sunderland supporters saw saves like that frequently from him. On the previous occasion Sunderland won the FA Cup in 1937, teenager Johnny Mapson set a record that still stands as the youngest cup winning goalkeeper. The stories of Sunderland's last line of defence is a book in its own right, and L R Roose's place within the pantheon of Black Cat goalkeepers is assured. He was one of the game's great goalkeepers and great characters, and at Sunderland we are proud to be listed as one of the Prince's clubs."

It's not only supporters who are waking up to Leigh Roose and the immense contribution that he made to the sport. Goalkeepers, both active and retired, are thinkers. They have a reputation for being students of the game and its history. They read books, not a pastime you tend to associate with football players. Perhaps more than anything, goalkeepers like to study other goalkeepers – dead or alive – to find out about their backgrounds, what made them tick, their techniques in training and match situations, what they did away from the game to relax, etc. As Leigh Roose finally emerges from the shadows, so the goalkeeping union is starting to regard him as a year zero figure.

"I love reading about Bert Trautmann, Frank Swift and people like that, but Leigh goes well back before even them," says Neville Southall, a man with 92 Welsh caps and 751 appearances for Everton behind him. "He was a pioneer, self-taught, relying on his instinct to learn and get things right. Instead of being reactive, he was proactive, which I rather like. He had a decent set of morals, a love of football and a love for life. He was obviously very, very good not to mention consistent because you don't get to play for those sorts of clubs and win that many caps if you're not. And he was also brave because going out there, at that time, with nothing really to protect you took some doing. It's quite nice to know that he was doing what I did, playing for my country, playing for a club I love, all that time ago. If it hadn't been for him then goalkeeping wouldn't be what it is now, but I'm not so sure whether he'd like the game today. The whole attitude has changed. Yeah, he got his money, but he also had morals. How can you pick up a hundred grand a week for doing something that you love and is so easy? He was someone with a medical background. That says a lot. He cared about stuff. He understood that you played for the love of it, not because it's a job. It's not a fair day's pay for a fair day's work anymore. That's why football has gone corporate and lost touch with its working class roots."

There's also an appreciation that the bravery displayed by Leigh and many other goalkeepers of his generation extended way beyond the football field into something far darker during World War One. "What makes you climb out of a trench and run towards a machine gun knowing that you are almost certainly going to die?" adds Neville. "The more you think about it, the madder it gets, and yet they did it. You've got to be a special person to be able to do that. In my heart, given the same circumstances, I'm not 100 per cent sure I'd do it. I suppose to begin with everyone was joining up thinking it was going to be over by Christmas, then they got there and realised 'Shit, I've got to go and do this now'. People say it's a nasty old world today, but think about what they went through and it wasn't exactly a barrel of laughs back then. Does mankind ever learn? Not from where I'm standing."

The fields sandwiched between the two roads leading north-west and north-east out of Gueudecourt across which Leigh and his comrades charged on the afternoon of Saturday 7 October 1916 now stand peaceful. The guns and soldiers may be long gone but the topography of the landscape remains essentially the same, with the scar of what was once Bayonet Trench clearly visible. It's still possible, all these years later, to visualise what happened here which makes Gueudecourt a place well worth visiting. And if your emotions threaten to spill over, you know what to do – visit that set of goalposts on the triangular green at the heart of the village and swing for a few seconds on the crossbar. It's what Leigh would have done.

The Making of a Player – Goalkeeping

I N 1906 Leigh was commissioned to write an article explaining in layman's terms what constitutes a good goalkeeper. The article was one of a series written by people within the game for a magazine rather misleadingly called *The Book of Football*. These were eventually compiled and released as a book, with Leigh's contribution forming a chapter called 'The Making of a Player – Goalkeeping'.

Much of what Leigh included in his article had already appeared in print virtually word for word courtesy of his columns in newspapers such as the *Daily Mail*, *The London Standard* and the *Football Evening News*. That didn't prevent the piece from being regarded at the time as the nearest thing there was to a goalkeeping manual, explaining why copies of it could still be found circulating around football clubs up until the late 1920s.

Despite the request by the publisher to write in layman's terms some of the language used by Leigh is somewhat erudite or, to borrow Dick Jenkins' expression from Chapter

Four, "quite highbrow." And while Leigh may have had a reputation as a sought after writer, there's no denying that his prose don't always make perfect sense. However, it's still a fascinating read. What follows is the article in full as it appeared in print back in 1906:

≪-≫

A GOOD goalkeeper, like a poet, is born, not made. Nature has all to do with the art in its perfection, yet very much can be done by early training, tuition and practice. A 'Natural' goalkeeper seems to keep his form without much effort. All the training possible will not make a man a goalkeeper. You must coach him, explain the finer points of the game to him, and show him the easiest and best way to take the ball to the greatest advantage, and how to meet this or that movement of the attacking forwards, and then he will be something more than a mere physical entity or specimen. Granted that the aspirant has the inherent and essential qualities in him to become successful, it is the early work and coaching that are the determining causes of after success, without which he can never hope to attain the ideal.

In the other positions in the field success is dependent upon combined effort and upon the dovetailing of one player's work with another. With the goalkeeper it is a different matter entirely. He has to fill a position in which the principle is forced upon him that 'it is good for a man to be alone' – a position which is distinctly personal and decidedly individualistic in character. His is the most onerous post, and one which is equally responsible. Any other player's mistakes may be readily excused, but a single slip on the part of the last line of defence may be classed among the list of the unpardonable sins – especially when the International Selection Committee is on business bent. His one mistake or lapse may prove more costly than a score of errors committed by all his fellow clubmates put together.

Nevertheless, a goalkeeper's position is a most fascinating one to take up, and the intense application which an aspirant willingly gives to it is the best proof of the powerful attraction of the duties incumbent on one filling that post. The attraction of 'paddling one's own canoe', as it were, in this pastime is equally pronounced as in the orthodox river pastime itself.

To prove a successful goalkeeper, a man must be one of those destined by nature to be 'on his own', as the resources for reliably filling the post are entirely in himself; and, unless he wishes to be purely imitative, the goalkeeper, like the silkworm, must produce his materials from himself. He must not even have a nodding acquaintance with 'nerves', the bête noire of many a man who otherwise would have been successful. The responsibility which it involves and entails should not have a tendency to make him feel timid otherwise he must give up the idea of ever excelling. He should be full of pluck, as in a very short time experience will teach him that an ounce of that genuine and useful attribute is worth a ton of the elusive element known as luck. Individually he should be extremely keen, and his physical agility should be commensurate with his mental alertness.

Goalkeeping is looked upon as the easiest position to take upon one's self in the field. The belief is as erroneous as it is common, and those people who suggest such betray gross ignorance. Certainly there are occasions when the goalkeeper has nothing more to do than support his own frame and weight, yet even then the routine and monotony are positively irksome to those whose preference is for something more than the 'simple life' from the keeper's point of view, and on such occasions they scarcely put credence in the sentiments contained in the phrase that 'they also serve who only stand and wait'.

It is this long waiting for shots that tries a goalkeeper – this watching and waiting when you see your forwards and backs being slowly but surely driven in on you that will make a man unsteady at the critical moment. Only those who have followed an important cup-tie from start to finish can appreciate the strain on the nerves of the spectators. What must it be, then, to the players engaged, particularly the goalkeeper? No doubt a good deal depends on temperament, but even the most light-hearted and careless acknowledge that the mental tension is severe, and when there is not much to occupy a goalkeeper's attention, what John Stuart Mill called 'the disastrous feeling that nothing matters' is apt to creep over the best of custodians when the spur is removed and the keenness taken away or only present after long intervals.

Only those who are active votaries rather than passive critics can appreciate the merit or the charm of goalkeeping, and such expect to find a little originality concurrent with that which we see brought to bear upon other games of skill. Everything that the aspirant to first-class rank attempts to accomplish should be marked by a steady, quiet confidence. There should be nothing to denote the novice about his play, albeit a champion in embryo. As a rule, men are clever at a game because they are fond of it, and when a man is fond of anything in which he takes part, he does not usually or as a rule scamp such work as he participates in.

Players with intelligence to devise a new move or system, and application to carry it out, will go far. And for that reason the possession of personal conception and execution is desirable, although a 'player with an opinion' nowadays which is not in consonance with the stereotyped methods of finessing and working for openings is shunned to no small degree, as though he carried about with him the germs of an infectious disease.

A goalkeeper, however, can be a law unto himself in the matter of his defence. He need not set out to keep goal on the usual stereotyped lines. He is at liberty to cultivate originality and, more often than not, if he has a variety of methods in his clearances and means of getting rid of the ball, he will confound and puzzle the attacking forwards.

Trickiness and ability to dodge an opponent are as absolutely necessary to a goalkeeper's art as that of a boxer should feint with his right and deliver a blow with his left. A custodian should confound his opponents when hard pressed by clearing exactly similar shots in totally different ways, and should not allow them to decide or guess by mere theory how he will act in getting rid of the ball or in clearing. He should 'bounce' the forwards, but keep it within proper limits.

A goalkeeper should be one possessed of acute observation and independent thought. He should be aggressive, and have the fighting instinct or spirit in him, and if in combination with a modicum of 'temper' – so called – he will be none the worse for that. Temper is only a form of energy and, so long as it is controlled, the more we have of it in a custodian the better. He should know every move of the game as well as he knows the alphabet, and study the mysteries of attack and the intricacies of defence, at the same time carrying his individual attitude with perfect balance. If he can give to his work the spice of a little originality, it will prove to be his advantage. Stale minds rather than stale bodies and muscles are responsible for many of the indifferent displays we read of. When a person's mannerisms seem part of the man, unconscious and necessary to the full self-expression of his work or play, it is folly to attempt to cramp one's methods for the sake of conformity to a general type. When, however, they are foreign to his role, they become a just source of irritation, and the reason for their adoption is possibly found in the fact that the person who has aped somebody's methods, which were in turn sub-aped by others, was suffering at both extremities of his person in that he was the possessor of a swollen head and had grown too big for his boots.

The fairest judgement of a man is by the standard of his work, and the best goalkeeper is the one who makes the fewest mistakes. Perfect custodians are not in evidence in this mundane sphere. There certainly are degrees of comparison in the best of goalkeepers, albeit of a limited kind, as the tactics indulged in by keepers are merely matters of personal equation.

Some men are born great, others achieve greatness, others have greatness thrust upon them. A goalkeeper may be of all these, but the best keepers are principally the first. They are expected to be perfection personified in their form – never to lapse or even make a mistake, and to possess all the virtues of the man who was sorry he had only the Ten Commandments to keep and no more. Granted perfection is desirable, but it is usually presentable only to the imagination in this imperfect world.

Let a goalkeeper be successful in his clearances, and great will be his triumph. Let him fail, and oblivion will be his portion. Orthodox views to the contrary notwithstanding, a goalkeeper and his methods of defence are the result of the physical make-up of the individual. This relative truth no one need gainsay. He should stand about six feet and no nonsense. Size gives one the impression of strength and safety, and enables a goalkeeper to deal with high and wide shots with comparative ease where a smaller or shorter man would be handicapped. On the other hand, a tall and ponderous goalkeeper is at a disadvantage with the smaller and more agile rival when required to get down to swift ground or low shots.

To the agility of youth should be coupled the sagacity of veterancy. His first duty, and, indeed, the primary responsibility incumbent upon him, is to ensure his team against defeat, and he should always play the game that is calculated to be most effectual in obviating defeat for his side. He should not be one of those incapable of anything of the ordinary, but should be able to rise to the occasion when such is demanded of him; otherwise, even if his critical friends are unable to locate any particular weakness, there will be feelings of unreliability somewhere in connection with his work.

The plans which he has in his head should be carried out unhesitatingly, and he should try to make himself fit naturally into the team's fabric. To be on the tip-toe of expectancy is a quality necessary in a top-grade custodian. Like the figure of Aunt Sally on a fair green, he is there for any of the opposition to take a cheap shy at him when, how, and from what position they please.

The manner in which some forwards score from unexpected positions and are successful at long range shows not only how often it is possible for a goalkeeper to be unsighted in the line of fire but, on the other hand, it is a striking illustration of the forward's well developed, natural abilities for taking in a position at a glance, and the defence is not found to be of the calibre supposed against such incisive attacks.

A keeper should be thoroughly in union with his backs, and thereby not only make his own work easier but help them to play better. If he is what is called a natural custodian, he will soon fit in with the defence's natural fabric, and there will be a blend of style which does not suggest to the spectator the idea of being put together 'at twice' and where the establishment of a clearing house for adjusting differences should be requisitioned. There should be combination in defence just as well as in attack, and a complete understanding.

A class back will not merely rush an opponent and spoil his progress. He will time his tackle so as to yield the best opportunity to enable him or his goalkeeper to capture the ball and place it to the best advantage. Neither should get rid of the ball in haphazard fashion, unless in exceptional instances. They should 'sweep the horizon' for the best spot to place the ball, probably to an unmarked forward who stands an excellent chance, or has opportunity to make good headway and, in course of time, such a defence will make the best attack appear not quite the deadly article they imagined, presuming the defenders have the ability to accept the opportunity consequent on the opposing forward's mistakes or finnicking methods. The tendency of the present day with forwards is to over-elaboration and excessive finessing for positions in the vicinity of the goal, with the inevitable result that their combined movements, carried out almost on draught-board lines, have proved ineffective against the timely virile and robust opposition to be encountered.

There is too much mere trifling, unprofitable fiddling about for nothing in the forward's game. Players are not allowed a certain time, as in chess, to decide upon a move, and immediate action should be taken by a forward in front of goal, and then would goal-scoring be much more frequent than at present.

There is a speculative element in every goalkeeper's venture from under his posts. Leaving one's goal is looked upon as a cardinal sin by those armchair critics who tell a goalkeeper what he should do and what he should not do, and administer advice from the philosophic atmosphere of the grand stand. They wobble mentally, in proportion with the custodian's success or want of success in rushing out to meet an opponent even when the result is as inevitable as when a man's logic is pitted against a woman's tears. A goalkeeper should take in the position at once and at a glance and, if deemed necessary, come out of his goal immediately, even if things were not what they at first seemed. Never more than in this case is it true that he who hesitates is lost. He must be regardless of his personal consequences and, if necessary, go head first into the pack into which many men would hesitate to insert a foot, and take the consequent gruelling like a Spartan. I am convinced that the reason why goalkeepers don't come out of their goal more often is their regard for personal consequences. If a forward has to be met and charged down, do not hesitate to charge with all your might. If you rush out with the intention of kicking, don't draw back but Kick (with a capital K!) at once.

If a thing is worth doing at all, it is worth doing properly and with all one's energy, and he who gives hard knocks must be prepared to accept hard knocks in return. A goalkeeper should believe in himself. If you don't have the confidence, it is a moral certainty your backs cannot, and their play will show it by lying close to goal and doing most of your work. As a consequence of this, the half-backs have too much defence thrown upon them, and are thus hampered, and cannot feed their forwards, so that there

THE MAKING OF A PLAYER – GOALKEEPING

is a weak display all round which takes its origin from the defects of one man, and a want of confidence in the last defensive unit on the side.

Consistency should be aimed at. The goalkeeper on whom you cannot rely or depend is like a man to whom you ask an inconvenient question, and who prevaricates in his answer. He should not be one of those who 'keep' one day with extreme brilliance, and another day make repeated and egregious mistakes. His work should be notable for its uniformity and in distinct contrast to the curate's egg, which was found to be good only in parts.

Real power in a goalkeeper is indicated by a combination of mental and physical skill. Separately the qualities are of great personal worth, but combined they undoubtedly characterise genius, and if a genius for guarding a goal shows itself in a young player, he is bound to come to the front. Goalkeeping is not only a physical exercise, but a moral discipline when looked upon in its true light and from a right and proper standpoint. It develops courage, perseverance, endurance and other qualities which fit one for fighting the battle of life. It is an education both of body and mind. For the position a 'mens sana in corpore sano' is requisite. Nothing is impossible, and inability to accept an opportunity consequent upon some hesitancy has often been the cause of a goalkeeper failing by a few inches, or the proverbial coat of varnish, to reach what would at one time have been a chance.

The goalkeeper's position tends to keep one's energies on the stretch, and it comes in the list of those pastimes, participation in which makes a man far younger when he arrives in the suburbs of the fifties than if he had in his youth dawdled over roses or dozed over parish magazines. Goalkeeping will take it out of a man if his heart is not in the game, and will soon kill his enthusiasm. On the other hand, if he is attracted to his position until it becomes part and parcel of his nature, he will guard his lines until he is ready to drop or collapse like a concertina.

Every clearance should be destined to do something, and every return quick. The custodian should never make capital out of any doubtful point, for though he be eager to win he should be still more determined to win like a sportsman. He will be kicked here, there and everywhere but should be content with appeals to the referee, and not take the law into his own hands. He should never appeal for anything he considers to be unfair. Appeals by the goalkeeper have had value, but he is scarcely the best man for the same. When granting a free to the opposition within scoring distance from goal, the referee should hint to the goalkeeper the nature of the free kick given, as it may be granted for one of those offences in respect of which the ball must be played by a second party before the shot would be allowed to count. It would be a great benefit if referees generally would adopt a 'double' whistle for a free kick from which a goal could not be scored direct, and it would tend to simplify matters, especially for goalkeepers as some referees with extensive knowledge give equally peculiar decisions; and it would need a desperate surgical operation of the sort suggested by Sydney Smith to introduce the why and the wherefore of these decisions very often, even to the most receptive intelligence.

If a player has the ability to keep goal, he should set about trying to improve his style. He may possibly be a little unfinished at first, but he is bound to improve if he combines with the agility of youth a matured observation of the game which time alone can give. A sure eye, a perfect sense of time, and a heart – even as big as a hyacinth farm

– are necessary to a goalkeeper's art, for it is an art of the rarest type. He should be as light on his feet as a dancing master, yet nothing is more reprehensible in a goalkeeper than taking wild, flying kicks, or using his feet in any way when he can use his hands, as there is safety in numbers and two hands are better than one foot. When he does kick, his kicking should be accuracy itself, so as to land the ball exactly where he intends. There must be boot behind the ball, muscle behind the boot, the intelligence behind both. He should be as cool as the proverbial cucumber, and good temper is an essential. Excitability and an uncontrollable disposition or temper are antagonistic to good judgement, and the goalkeeper who is devoid of judgement is useless for all practical purposes.

If a player is mapping out a goalkeeper's career for himself, his course should be one of moderation, regularity, and simplicity. Nothing is ever achieved without effort or even sacrifice in one's pastimes, as in the higher walks of life, and only a study of its points and experience will educate him up to the standard expected of him. Let a player take that for granted, and he will succeed.

Bibliography

Corrigan, Peter: *100 Years of Welsh Soccer* (Welsh Brewers Ltd, 1975)

Hazlewood, Nick: *In the Way! Goalkeepers: A Breed Apart* (Mainstream Publishing, 1998)

Hutchinson, Roger: *Into the Light – A Complete History of Sunderland Football Club* (Mainstream Publishing, 1999)

O'Neill, Herbert Charles: *The Royal Fusiliers in the Great War* (Naval & Military Press, 1922)

Stead, Peter & Richards, Huw: *For Club and Country: Welsh Football Greats* (University of Wales Press, 2000)

Toulmin, Vanessa: *The Electric Edwardians: The Films of Mitchell and Kenyon* (British Film Institute, 2004)

Ward, Andrew: *Football's Strangest Matches* (Robson Books, 1999)